Praise for *Turning Toward Grief*

"This book is gentle, affirming company on the path of grieving. It doesn't shy away from the pain, the work, the time that grief requires of us, but it does remind us that we have power and agency on our journey toward healing."

—**Jarod K. Anderson**, author of *Something in the Woods Loves You*

"James Crews's poetry is such a gift to the heart. Opening this book is a gentle way to tend to our wounds, soothe our soul, and remind us that grief, too, nourishes and feeds us. Perhaps most importantly, the words on these pages remind us that we are not alone in our grief. Grateful for every second spent with these poems and prompts!"

—**Meryl Arnett**, meditation teacher, and the creator of *Our Mindful Nature* podcast

"In *Turning Toward Grief*, James Crews tenderly invites his fellow grievers in for a slow softening of the heart. Each poem and prompt is an outstretched hand that offers an 'of course . . .' His words—so personal and universal—inspire inner wisdom and offer the medicine of witness, a potent salve to loss. With ease, Crews challenges the spell of separateness, allowing folks to see themselves through his words, as they work their magic, nudging the grief explorer to dare to peek a little deeper into the caverns of loss."

—**Tracy Chalmers and Willow Meili**,
cofounders of The Grief Well

"*Turning Toward Grief* is a gentle invitation to face heartbreak and to wrestle with adversity. James Crews invites readers to approach even further: to see grief as an opportunity for growth, creativity, and action. His poems are rich, real, and raw. And he incorporates short essays and writing prompts that inspire us to craft our own narratives of love and loss."

—**Andrew Ingall**, director of virtual
public programs, Reimagine

"In *Turning Toward Grief,* James Crews writes with the honesty and tenderness of someone who knows grief intimately. His words comfort without platitudes and companion without judgment. Through poems, essays, and writing prompts, Crews offers both solace and creative practices to accompany those navigating sorrow. His prompts encourage a deep listening: to memory, to ourselves, and to the enduring presence of love. This book is not only a companion in grief, but a testament to the beauty that persists even in the face of unimaginable loss."

—**Alix Klingenberg**, author of *Quietly Wild: Poems, Photographs, and Rituals to Mark the Seasons*

"James Crews offers us a wealth of model poems and short essays, followed by an invitation to write our own, imploring us to discover our complex responses to various aspects of loss and grief. But he also includes encouragement to write about themes of love and appreciation, making this a book that feels balanced and whole, a book unique in its approach to making sense of ourselves in the face of the unknowable, as well as in its sense of understanding and appreciation for the mysteries and poetry of being human."

—**Dorianne Laux**, author of *Life on Earth* and Pulitzer Prize finalist

"*Turning Toward Grief* is a warm invitation inviting us to write and reflect on the messiness—and complexity—that grief demands. With deep love, Crews weaves the brokenness, searching, yearning, and need for connection that shadow our daily lives in the aftermath of loss. He braids these threads with glimmers of light, softening yesterday's pain, all the while reminding us that we are not alone."

—**Joyal Mulheron**, founder and executive director of Evermore

"Many turn from hard things, but some have learned the trick of tropism toward the difficult—swiveling to face down what stings. By this habit, when loss brings grief, grief can kindle creation. Grief can be the muse. James Crews has long consoled us with his poems and anthologies to companion our troubles and joys. In this book he turns toward grief to offer a triple gift: poems, meditations, and prompts for healing."

—**Kim Stafford**, author of *As the Sky Begins to Change*

"In *Turning Toward Grief*, James Crews invites us into his careful exploration of personal loss and great pain, while weaving universal experiences of grief into every line. This is what his accessible language does best—it creates community and welcomes everyone to engage. This is a book that reminds us how to care for one another through hardship and reflects the beauty of our brokenness. This work is 'unafraid to show affection, here to let you know / you're not alone.' Crews asks us to look directly at grief, to turn toward it with tenderness and attention, accepting that 'there is no cure for the ache of aliveness.' These poems, reflections, and prompts are portals that unfurl our layers of healing, uncovering pathways for slow and sacred transformation, allowing grief to be a divine and connective guide."

—**Jacqueline Suskin**, author of *The Verse for Now*

"I can think of no better guide into the intimate landscapes of loss than James Crews. With his signature gentleness, wisdom, clarity, and compassion, he gives voice to the nuances of grief, shares his own healing process, and invites the reader to explore their own tender experiences of grief and love. If a book could hold your hand and say, 'You're not alone—I'm here,' this one would."

—**Rosemerry Wahtola Trommer**, author of *The Unfolding* and host of *The Poetic Path*

"As a bereavement and end-of-life therapist, I have long waited for a book like *Turning Toward Grief* to be written. Filled with poems and invitations to reflect or write, *Turning Toward Grief* will offer you, in accessible language, the solace, deep companionship, and wisdom you need for your journey. With this book in hand, you can be assured unequivocally that you are not alone and that however you are grieving, you are doing it right."

—**Claire Willis**, author of *Lasting Words* and *Opening to Grief*

Turning Toward Grief

Turning Toward Grief

Reflections on Life, Loss, and Appreciation

James Crews

BROADLEAF BOOKS
MINNEAPOLIS

TURNING TOWARD GRIEF
Reflections on Life, Loss, and Appreciation

Copyright © 2025 James Crews. The author has retained all reprint rights for the poems published in this book. Published by Broadleaf Books. All rights reserved. Except for brief quotations in critical articles or reviews, no part of this book may be reproduced in any manner without prior written permission from the publisher. Email copyright@broadleafbooks.com or write to Permissions, Broadleaf Books, PO Box 1209, Minneapolis, MN 55440-1209.

30 29 28 27 26 25   1 2 3 4 5 6 7 8 9

Library of Congress Control Number: 2025000992 (print)

Cover design by Broadleaf Books
Cover image © 2025 Getty Images; Seamless pattern with pink lilies/1178089380 by Aksiniya_Polyarnaya

Print ISBN: 979-8-8898-3415-1
eBook ISBN: 979-8-8898-3416-8

Printed in China.

Dedicated to the memory of my mother,
father, and grandmothers. May your
spirits rest in peace and joy.

Life is not about "or"—it is about "and." It is magical and messy, heartwarming and heartbreaking. It is delight and disappointment. Grace and grief. Exquisite and excruciating, often at the exact same time.

—Kristi Nelson

Contents

Introduction	1
Kintsugi Again	7
Stay Like Clay	11
Wound	15
Follow Your Grief	19
Made Visible	23
Finding My Mother	27
Phone Call	31
New Year	35
Caregiver	39
The Longest Journey	43
Forgotten Church	47
How to Love Yourself	51
All I Want	55
Staying Open	59

Spring Equinox	63
The First Peony	67
Summer Solstice	71
Compassion	75
Gentle	79
To Be Alive	83
Small Wonder	87
A Slice of Actual Light	91
A Bowl of Hydrangeas	95
Early October	99
Like the Trees	103
Like the Fern	107
Tenderness	111
How to Listen	115
How to Comfort Someone	119
In a Friend's Garden	123
Blue-Eyed Grass	127
So Much Space for Song	131
Say Yes	135
A Better Place	139
Strict Diet	143
Ember	147

Pilot Light	151
For Now	155
The Clearing	159
Scarlet Tanager	163
Only Moments Matter	167
Glimmers	171
Sweet Mystery	175
Ache of Aliveness	179
Mother Light	183
Acknowledgments	187
Notes	191

Introduction

If given a choice, none of us would invite grief into our lives, if it came knocking, asking to be let in. But grief does not give us any warning. Before we know it, some sudden loss is already in the house, begging for our attention, beside us at every moment. Now we have a choice. We can ignore the pain, which means it will show up anyway down the road, or we can turn toward it now and listen to what it will teach us.

Having lost my father at the age of twenty, when he was just forty-three years old, I thought I knew a lot about grief. I thought I had learned sorrow's central lesson—to appreciate what we have, and the people we love, while they are still here. But a few decades after that devastating, life-altering death came the year when I lost both of my grandmothers, a beloved job as a university professor, and my mother, who died suddenly at the age of sixty-four. To say I was undone by the pain of this time is an understatement. I swam in my grief for months, though it felt more like flailing—at times enraged, at other times barely able to function. The loss of my mother proved a watershed moment in my life, and I realized I had forgotten that lesson from so long ago. I had been taking her for granted, believing things would always stay as they were.

What saved me during this difficult time was the kindness of others who showed up for me, the love and support of my husband, a good therapist, and my daily writing practice. On the morning after my mother died, I picked up my notebook and pen and simply let the words flow out, grateful I had a way to record how bewildered I felt in the wake of her death. In the weeks and months that followed, my writing became a refuge for me, as any creative practice can be in times of confusion. I was not writing well, since most of what came never made it beyond my notebook, but the writing was for myself alone. I did not share it with anyone, and it felt like a way to process my grief, as well as to keep the spirit of my mother alive. I recalled that grief was how I first came to poetry after my father died, and now here it was, saving me once again.

Because of its textured, complex nature, there is something about grief that can't be captured by everyday language. This is perhaps why we often bristle and cringe at the supposedly comforting phrases that other people offer us—because words fail in the face of the mystery that is death. Poetry, on the other hand, is built to hold uncertainty and contradiction, joy and sorrow, often at the same moment in time. It is the ideal vehicle for conveying the truth of how it feels to suffer a loss and what it's like when that suffering briefly lifts. This is why I felt called to write this book, gathering poems from the past few years that speak to the ever-shifting presence of grief in our lives, and including both reflections and prompts that build on each piece. Most of us do not turn to poetry on a daily basis, but when the unimaginable has happened, we go searching for words that don't feel hollow, words that strike at the heart of our loss. I invite each of you to use the poems collected here as jumping-off points for writing of your own, or even conversations with trusted loved ones. I invite you to step through whatever portals of memory they offer, perhaps seeking out a creative practice that speaks to you and allows the grief to move through—which is all it ever wants to do.

Working on this book, even years after that dark time, has not been easy. I often had to pause in the middle of my writing in order to regroup and heal the wounds that reopened in the process. I encourage you to do the same—read this book all at once, or little by little each day or week, whatever feels best tailored to your own process. Feel free to put it down and then come back later. For me, the never-ending journey of grief revolves around gentleness and self-care as we learn to turn toward our pain. It will be hard, but like a tulip that emerges through still-frozen soil, we can train ourselves to look for even the weakest rays of sun in the midst of our personal winter. This does not mean grief will evaporate, that we will not feel any more pain. And finding the light does not mean that we are dishonoring the ones we have lost. We deserve whatever joys and whispers of warmth we can find in the middle of all this. Let's agree not to beat ourselves up for laughing or feeling the lift of delight from some small thing. Turning toward grief means inviting inside the intensity of *all* our emotions to the table, even those we believe we're not supposed to feel while in mourning.

Our culture does not give us many resources for loss, so we can develop the false idea that after a certain point, we should be "over it," we should be "past it by now." You will see that many of the early poems and reflections here offer a different perspective, giving us all permission to "stay broken" for as long as we need to be, not rushing through fresh grief to reach some state of "repair." Sorrow only changes and shape-shifts over time, in any case. It never goes away completely, and I do not believe we ever reach a point where we are fully healed. Most of us, on reflection, probably would not give up our grief if given the chance. It is a direct line back to our loved one, back to their life, and it is a threshold into deeper appreciation of every moment of our lives. Only we can decide whether or not we step through.

Above all, I hope these poems and reflections show there is no right or wrong way to grieve, no matter what people will try to tell us (and so many will try). Only we can find the rituals and practices that will support us in this raw and vulnerable time. I am no expert on grief. I can only offer what was spoken to me through these poems—truths, memories, insights, and expressions of pain that have carried me through. Over twenty years ago, when my father died from complications of hepatitis C, I was just a kid. I can forgive myself for turning away from my grief back then and embracing instead what was available at the time to dull the ache—alcohol, cigarettes, drugs, and long nights spent at bars just trying to run from the reality that my father, who could once fix anything, was now gone. The more I pushed down my pain, stuffing it away, the more it came out in other ways over the years, prolonging the process. Following the terrible loss of my mother, for whom I was a caregiver for most of my life, I made a deal with myself: I would feel *everything* and do my best not to run from the suffering. I would try to stay open. There is no sugarcoating it—this decision brought on several deep depressions I thought I'd never recover from. Yet even in that difficult time, I found many glimmers, gaps between the bouts of unbearable grief. Even a patch of winter light rising up and down the wall one evening promised me some measure of solace. You will make it through this, it said. You will find beauty again.

Kintsugi Again

In the Japanese art of mending ceramics
with powdered gold, no one ever
talks about how they'd leave the pots,
cups, and cracked bowls broken
for a while, sometimes whole generations.
And so I say to you: Let your heart stay
shattered in your chest, let it ache.
Some may claim you've now been
broken open, and can let in the light.
This might be true, but before you rush
to gloss over the wounds, filling
the holes with gold so they glimmer,
try to find beauty in the broken places too,
proof of where the fire left its marks on you.

When we find ourselves broken by fresh grief, others will rush in to comfort us, offering what words they can. More than once, some well-meaning friend has tried to give me solace in the midst of sorrow by pointing out that my heart may be broken, but it is also *broken open*. I feel this is true of any pain we are able to stay with—that it opens us more to love, life, and the whole overwhelming world. Yet I also think that as a culture, we move too fast toward healing, usually before we have even had a chance to sit with our brokenness and let it change us as it must. I have been guilty myself of searching so hard for the silver lining in a difficult situation, I ignore the storm that must pass through me and do its work. Perhaps that's why this poem came to me one morning during a long walk about a year after my mother had died. I usually prefer to write in a notebook at my desk before dawn each morning, but the words of this poem insisted on being taken down so much that I had to pull out my phone and type it all right at that moment. I had been thinking about the words of those well-meaning friends and the way the Japanese practice of kintsugi—filling the cracks in pottery with powdered gold—has become such a commonplace metaphor for the ways we treat our trauma and pain. But I also remembered that a friend told me recently that's only *part* of the practice. Often, in kintsugi, the pieces of pottery are allowed to stay broken for a long time, even whole generations, before they are finally repaired with gold. This begs the question: Can we give ourselves the same permission to stay in grief or despair for as long as we need to, before rushing to try to fix it, before allowing others to talk us out of the pain we know we need to grow?

Invitation for Writing & Reflection: How do you find beauty in the broken places? How might you relate to the Japanese practice of kintsugi, and in what ways does this metaphor of repairing cracks with gold apply to your own grief right now?

Stay Like Clay

How we want hard things to soften
and change right away, for frost
to lift off stiff blades of grass
before the summer green can fade,
and for a gentle rain to prevail over
sleet that coats each leaf left
clinging to gleaming black branches.
For the furrowed brow of a loved one
to smooth back into a smile,
and for every clenched fist to unfurl
into a small bowl, ready to hold
whatever small thing falls inside.
Maybe the trick is never to harden
in the first place, to stay like clay
outside the kiln, willing to be
molded, reshaped by the rough
and tender hands of this world.

It seems a lot to ask of any of us dealing with loss to stay as pliable as clay, not hardening into bitterness, anger, or resentment. In a way, it makes sense that we might choose to harden and armor ourselves against a world as rough and tender as this one, where sudden change without warning is often the rule. Of course, we feel the need to protect ourselves, guard our hearts against breaking in the face of so much grief, suffering, and pain. But hardening only harms us, and those around us, keeping us from feeling deeply what only wants to pass through. It might feel impossible now, but maybe we can eventually come to see the hands of grief molding and reshaping us into more compassionate and caring souls, awake to moments of aliveness that we cherish. Perhaps we are learning how to hold what is true right now, how to notice the frosted blades of grass and a battering sleet, how to receive each wave of sorrow, without wishing it away, without trying to relive and revise the past so that things might have turned out differently. "Staying like clay" is the deep work for each of us as we turn toward this grief—choosing not to resist reality whenever we can and instead allowing ourselves to be reshaped by the ever-shifting hands of our new circumstances. This is how we stay open to the possibility of joy again, how we might reignite our own purpose. This is how we make the radical choice of inner peace, which always begins with the unfurling of our own tightly clenched fists. In this way, maybe sensing that we have the soft blessing of our loved one, we might signal to the world: I am ready to live again a little; I am ready to be changed.

Invitation for Writing & Reflection: Consider some of the ways you might have hardened against your grief, and the outer world. What would it mean for you to "stay like clay," to soften into what's true for you at this moment? You might begin with my first line, "How we want hard things to soften," and see what images come to you.

Wound

Sometimes, a wound
must stay a wound.
No balm to calm the ache,
no charms against the evil
that harmed. To grieve
is to live with the pain,
as you sit by the bedside
of an ailing relative,
your hand held out
across the white blanket
for when they are ready
to grasp and squeeze.
Even if that means
the hand must stay
empty for a while.

The people in our lives who struggle to hold our grief
with us will often push us to move on, perhaps long

before we are ready. As the daily rituals and routines of life resume, we might do this to ourselves too, rushing ahead long before we are ready. Yet if we are to let grief pass freely through us, our wound must stay a wound for a while. We cannot stitch together an injury that has not finished bleeding, nor can we erase the cracks in our soul that will need a great deal of attention to heal. Perhaps we know what it is like to sit with an ailing loved one as they fight for each breath, clinging to the last embers of life left within them. We may know what it is like to hold out a hand, hoping to offer something, only to have them refuse the comfort, unable to receive it. In the same way, we must now sit by the bedside of our own pain, making peace with the fact that our hands may stay empty for a while. There may be nothing that fixes this. We might have felt more useful and productive when our loved one was still alive and there was so much to take care of. It can unsettle us to have nothing left to do, to feel so "useless" in the face of grief. Yet think of how helpful we felt by simply being present with our loved one close to the end, if we had that privilege, or what a comfort it was to share some simple moment of sitting together, not doing much at all. Our only job now is to allow our wounds to ache as they will, exposing them to light and air so they can begin to mend. It is not self-indulgent to stay with the pain, to leave room for grief in every moment it arises. Just as we show up for others in their darkest hours, we can be there for ourselves as well. We can admit that we are the wounded ones who now require tenderness and care.

Invitation for Writing & Reflection: What are some of the ways you can allow your pain to stay as it is right now, refusing the advice of others who might rush you to move on? How might you sit beside your own grief, keeping vigil over yourself at this tender and difficult time? What small things might you offer yourself right now?

Follow Your Grief

> Everyone says to follow your bliss,
> but what if, some days, you need
> to pull the shades, draw the covers
> over your head, and turn toward
> grief instead? What if sadness calls
> like the one candle left burning
> in a room, with its blackened wick,
> its scent of struck matches, and flicker
> of long-gone breath? Joy is the fire
> we're taught never to deny, but why
> not see sorrow as elemental too—
> plunging both hands deep into that
> rich, black soil in which anything,
> anything might grow?

It may seem counterintuitive—even risky—to follow the call of our grief, especially when it is inconvenient or embarrassing. We may spend months or years denying how we really feel, trying to fit into a culture that tells us over and over to follow our bliss. Others may encourage us to gloss past the depth of our pain and paint it over with the veneer of false happiness. It's true that joy, if followed, can lead us where we need to be. But turning away from our grief, that lone candle left burning, also shuts off our access to positive emotions like joy, delight, and wonder. It will perhaps feel self-indulgent not to answer phone calls or messages for a time, not to answer the door, or call into work—but in these shaky early days, our self-care must come first. We never want to sugarcoat the presence of sorrow in our life or anyone else's, yet many of us know from experience that even the darkness of grief contains possibility. A strange uplift can come on the other side of giving ourselves over to the waves of sadness when they come. Grief asks us to plunge both hands deep into the soil of this awful, new experience, in which we may discover traces of a new path. We never would have asked for this and do not willingly turn toward it. Yet maybe we can see that loss has given us a chance to remake our life, to decide how we want to move through the world. It may come only as a flicker at first, but even that hint of possibility can light our way.

Invitation for Writing & Reflection: What would it mean right now for you to follow your grief, to give in when it calls for your gentle attention? Can you trust that, even though you may not feel it now, every sorrow holds a hint of possibility? If you choose to write, you might begin with the phrase "Today I need to" and see what unseen needs arise that might have been living at the edges of your awareness.

Made Visible

> Some days I wish our pain was visible,
> that our grief gave off a slight glimmer
> from the center of the chest, so that as we
> walked down the street, shifting a bag
> of olive oil and bread from one hand
> to the other, every passerby might see
> a glow lifting off of us like moonlight
> on the surface of broken water, and know
> to soften their eyes, and whisper hello.

Wouldn't it be easier if the people we met already knew about our grief, if they could see a slight glimmer coming off of us and understand that our hearts had been broken? Then we would not have to explain it over and over to each new person, reopening the wounds. This can be one of the hardest passages of the grieving process—having to share the news of our fresh loss with others as we merge with the current of our lives again.

And there is nothing that can take away the sting of each retelling, no way for the rest of the world to see that we are in the grip of this pain, no matter how old or new it might be.

Yet perhaps knowing how our own deep grief has affected us, shifting our moods without warning, leaving us feeling off-center, we can extend kindness to everyone we meet. We can assume that they, too, have endured their own forms of heartache. We might even develop the uncanny ability to see beneath the surface of other people at times, to read the dark circles under their eyes or feel inside their weariness a similar, life-altering loss.

In general, however, we can never know the depths of another's grief simply by looking at them. We have to trust that death has touched the lives of literally everyone around us, whether directly or indirectly. Every household has felt that shadow pass through its doors. This does not ease our own pain entirely, of course, but while performing those ordinary tasks that can seem so trivial and surreal in the face of sudden loss—shopping for bread and olive oil, for instance—perhaps there is solace in knowing that what we feel is both personal *and* universal. We might wish others could see those glimmers of grief and greet us with more softness, yet if this were true, we would find that same glow lifting off the chests of everyone we know and every stranger on the planet.

Invitation for Writing & Reflection: Allowing yourself to speak from the place of your own deep grief, you might begin by writing "Some days I wish" and see what arises for you. Let the wish be wild or strange or sincere. In the face of this new pain, what do you wish that others could know simply on seeing you?

Finding My Mother

The day you passed away, I stumbled
along icy sidewalks, searching for any
sign of you, but felt only the crunch
of salt beneath my boots, breathed in only
the sting of diesel smoke and roasting coffee.
Then I looked up to find a young woman
walking in front of me, wearing your color—
her dark purple sweatshirt pulled over
a pair of skin-tight, light violet jeans—
and how could I not think you were
winking at me from wherever you are now,
sending this woman rushing into a cafe,
here then gone in a flash of the same
purple as your bedroom walls and sheets,
your towels, and the oversized nightshirts
you took to wearing at the end, becoming
your own burst of color there on the couch,
no matter how gray or lightless the day
might have seemed at first.

We will return over and over to those first moments, days, and weeks after our loved one's death, just as we will come back to those times just before we lost them. This period of our lives is, after all, imprinted on us and marks a major turning point—the instant when one world dissolved and a new one began for us. I was not with my mother when she died, and so the news came to me and my husband while in Montreal, where I'd traveled for work. I had some inkling of what was coming, having been told by relatives that she took a sudden turn and would not make it through the night. While I was not surprised to receive the call early the next morning, any death—no matter how anticipated, no matter that it means the end of a loved one's long suffering—comes as a total shock to the system.

As we walked the icy streets that morning and I listened to my husband sharing the news with his own mother on the phone, I felt lost, confused, untethered. But then, out of nowhere, a young woman appeared on the sidewalk in front of us, dressed head to toe in several shades of purple, my mother's favorite color. I could have easily called this encounter a coincidence, yet coming so closely as it did on the heels of her passing, it felt too obvious, too in-my-face, to turn away. Was she reaching out from wherever she is now to let me know she's still with me in some way? Or was this just my mind seeking to comfort itself with the first bit of solace and seeming connection that crossed my path? It did not matter to me. Inside the fresh grief of that moment, I would have taken any comfort I could find, any scrap of hope; and in the days that followed, there came many more such "winks" and visitations from beyond that were too jarring to simply shrug off.

This was when I learned one of the essential lessons of loss—never doubt what feels true to me, even if it seems illogical or strange to others. No one else is living through this sorrow as we are now, in our own particular ways, striking our own specific path. And if we believe our loved one is near, reaching out, sending us signs of their presence, we can trust that impulse as absolutely true. If we have had no contact or connection with our loved one since their death, that is also natural and true, just as it should be. We must remind ourselves that there is no right or wrong way to grieve or to remember; there is only the choice of whether or not we listen to our own experience of grief. The world is filled enough with so-called logic and easy explanation; now is the time to embrace our faith and to welcome the love-light that finds us, no matter how it shows up in our lives—a familiar phrase, the sound of a laugh, or some burst of color that reminds us of the one we have lost.

Invitation for Writing & Reflection: Describe your own experience of fresh grief, especially those moments before and after the loss of your loved one that most stay with you. Have you felt some "winks" from your loved one or a lack of connection since their death? Remembering that no experience is wrong or right, you might write about some encounter, no matter how small, that brought back the time you shared together.

Phone Call

The voice of my oldest friend
was as warm as the waves
of heat rippling from the top
of the cast-iron woodstove,
almost like a steady flame
I could carry in my pocket
and keep with me for the rest
of the blustery December day,
while I chopped carrots
into little suns that sizzled
in the oiled skillet, while I
swept the mudroom of dust
and gravel for the hundredth time,
giving it back to the ground
still tucked under layers of snow.
When she said *hello* today,
it was like stepping into the arms
of the same wool coat I've been
wearing for years, my worries

> lifting off as I slipped on
> the familiar cloth of words
> stretched between us.

In order to navigate the changed and challenging terrain of this new landscape we find ourselves in, we will need to lean on the strength of the people who know us best. Loss inevitably disrupts our connection to the larger world and those people who once sustained us on a daily basis. For a while, we may need to live in a kind of isolation, processing what has happened to us and waiting until we know who among our friends, family, and coworkers can receive and hold this grief with us in the ways that we need them to. We may, in fact, need to actively *choose* how and with whom we spend our precious time and energy, limited as it will be now. Most likely, we will find ourselves drawn most to those people—some of them surprising—who approach us with openness, without an agenda, and with whom we can be our full and shattered selves. Perhaps they are the ones who leave us food, offer to run errands, send us a heartfelt letter in the mail. Maybe they are the ones who show up at the door and are ready to sit with us in silence for as long as necessary, not trying to fix a single thing. Or as in the case of this poem, there might be an old friend or family member whose voice soothes you like no one else's, who knows you so completely it doesn't take an ounce of effort to talk with them. In fact, you feel held by their presence, able to slip on their affection like an old wool coat—durable, practical, and necessary for the winter you now face. The easy exchange of kindness between friends and loved ones can bring the same sense of sudden renewal as a fine dusting of snow, covering the colorless ground of our grief.

Invitation for Writing & Reflection: Describe a time when you reconnected with an old friend during an especially difficult period in your life. Even if your friend is no longer with us, you might write about what that relationship has meant to you. Begin with the phrase "The voice of my oldest friend" and see where that takes you as you consider the warmth and necessity of friendship, especially during this trying time.

New Year

It's so cold on this January morning
the condensation in the corner of each window
has frozen to the glass, cannot be wiped away.
But the woodstove's lit and breathing
like an animal asleep, giving off its heat.
I think of all the sorrows of this past year
as beads on a necklace that keep falling off,
the empty string still tied around my neck.

And yet—two of the most beautiful words
in the English language—sudden gratitude
rises up with each creak of the pine floorboards,
and swoop of the barred owl from tree to tree,
for staying alive to all this, even the blank
face of the silent phone, even the restless hours
before dawn, my eyes working much harder
but still somehow able to see in the dark.

Scientists have now proven that the daily practice of identifying at least three new things for which we feel grateful can keep us from slipping into depression and despair. This is partly because we learn to work the muscle of gratefulness even on those days when we don't especially feel like it, as in times of loss or struggle. All this may feel like cold comfort to those of us locked in the tight, airless space of grief where there seems to be no room for gratitude and nothing new to appreciate. For a while, it may be true that mourning is our main occupation. Yet even in times of darkness, we might find that a "sudden gratitude" arises naturally in us for just a few instants. Our practice then is not to ignore that sense of warmth for our own life, but to turn toward it instead. Yes, we feel the deep ache of missing our loved one and the irrevocable change in our circumstances; *and yet*, maybe the creak of the floorboards and the humming woodstove bring us back to our physical selves for an instant. Maybe the quick swoop of an owl from a snowy branch draws our attention elsewhere for a few seconds, and we let out a small gasp of awe.

I still remember quite vividly the New Year's Day after my mother's death that led to this poem, the morning so cold, condensation had frozen on the windows. The loss of my mother and both grandmothers felt like an empty string tied around my neck, so much missing from what had felt like such a full life just a year ago. I kept expecting my mother to call me, to leave a message once more saying that she needed my help with buying groceries online or making a doctor's appointment. I couldn't sleep, my world so altered it felt like the whole planet had tilted, ready to spill me off into space. And yet I also felt grateful for the stove that heated the house, for the woods in which we live, for the ways I still feel companioned by my mother, even when she is gone. So many emotions coexist in us, and they do not have to conflict. We may simply see them as part of a larger tapestry whose design we can only guess at. But staying present to our lives as they are now, to the pain as it arises, will help us feel our way through the darkness and confusion of this time. We will come to know ourselves as part of the cloth that holds everyone in relationship together.

Invitation for Writing & Reflection: Can you name at least three specific things that you feel grateful for right now? Try to be as granular as you can, not just listing family, house, and job, but instead identifying exactly what's allowing you even the smallest hint of appreciation for your life. Once you've found your three things, in your journal or in conversation with a trusted friend or family member, you might say why these specifics stand out to you as worthy of gratitude at this time.

Caregiver

You have put off all the small rituals
of care for the body, ignoring every ache
and pain of your own as just the pounding
of a passing storm. Now that your loved one
is gone, the rain won't stop, and you can
no longer deny that thunder and lightning
don't split the sky. Now, like a mother
to yourself, you rise from sleep in the night
to give food, give drink, give heat—pulling
the wool blanket over your feet. Now, you say
a resounding no to whatever gets in the way
of your love for this fierce and tender creature
you must caretake, lifting all the shades
in the house, and bringing a glass of cold
water to your lips, little by little coming back
to the only world there is.

Even if we were not actively taking care of someone we have now lost, no doubt we have used up a great deal of energy in grieving them. We may find ourselves doubly exhausted, especially when faced with the prospect of reentering the daily flow of life. Even after our loved one is gone, the harsh inner critic may tell us it is selfish to want to tend to our needs right now while we are supposed to be in mourning. We may also, at times, believe we don't deserve the kind of mothering described in this poem. It is a false and sometimes automatic assumption, but we can start to think that because our loved one has suffered and passed on, we must stay in pain too. Yet if we can keep a small group of caring individuals around us, they will likely reflect back to us—hopefully very gently—that it is time to pay attention to our own well-being again.

Our bodies themselves will let us know when we have strayed too far from self-care, and must once more give loving kindness to the fierce and tender creature we are. As the poem suggests, our gestures do not have to be grand; as we grieve, listening to our basic needs (so easily ignored in sorrow) will be more than enough. Sometimes, all we can manage is getting out of bed to pull aside the drapes or lift the shades. Sometimes, a simple glass of water and an extra blanket tugged over our feet are enough to remind us we are worthy of our own care. Giving ourselves food, drink, and heat—or whatever we need—signals to us: We belong to this world still, with all its physical pleasures and difficulties alike.

Invitation for Writing & Reflection: Has there been a period in your life when you ignored your own needs in service of caretaking someone else? How did it feel to come back from that, to return to some sense of self-care and presence to your own well-being?

The Longest Journey

You long to lead the life you love,
but fear the needful voices of others
crying out for you to fix their pain.
It can be the longest journey to reach up,
pull down the oxygen mask and strap it
to your own face, breathing in deeply
before helping another. But once you do,
once you feel the flow of air in your lungs,
like a necessary medicine that was
always available, always free, you see
how life wants to fill you too, and you can
refuse to be pulled back down into
that tight, airless place of emergency.
It is not selfish to relish your own breath,
to seek only the light that feeds you.

By now, we are all familiar with the metaphor of putting on our own oxygen masks—first looking after our own well-being—before we venture to help another. Yet this can seem like the longest journey, performing such actions of self-care, taking the time that we need, especially if we have spent months or even years as a caregiver. It becomes even more difficult if we must continue to care for others while also tending our own grief. I wrote this poem a few months before my mother died at a time when I felt exhausted and burned out from years of caretaking, all those phone calls, grocery orders, and doctors' appointments—the chores I'd now give anything to perform again. Looking back now, I believe I sensed that the most trying time was yet to come, and so these words came as a reminder that I could not be truly present for my mother unless I also took a break sometimes to breathe more deeply, finding small ways to stay attentive to my spirit as well.

Even during the last week we shared together at the hospital, I had to draw some boundaries. I never wanted to leave her, and she certainly begged me to stay, even when I stepped away to use the restroom. Yet I knew if I did not rest and refuel, I would not show up as fully the next day and the next. It almost became a mantra for me—*Not selfish, not selfish*—as I tore myself away from her bedside, away from her harshly lit room, the chapped and papery skin of her hand in mine. Sometimes, even a short walk on the grounds around the hospital, taking in the tall native grasses turning brown against the crisp, blue autumn sky, felt like a deep pull of the oxygen I needed to keep going.

It doesn't take much is another mantra from that time that helps as I heal into my grief, even years later. It doesn't take much to renew the weary spirit, to look after a body we may have neglected in the months before and after our loved one's passing. Some days, we have to make the longest journey and reach for whatever sources of light we can find in times of darkness. Once we do, once we keep reaching, the muscle only grows stronger, and the actions of self-compassion, however small, become more automatic as we feel the air flowing into our lungs again.

Invitation for Writing & Reflection: Make a list of things that you feel would be sources of light and air for you right now as you struggle through grief. Even if you are not able to practice *all* of them, see if you can do one or two things for yourself that might renew the spirit and give you at least a little room to breathe.

Forgotten Church

The next time you pray for someone else,
send whispered words on shaky wings
up to the night sky, you might consider
including yourself before the final amen.
When you ask for your own happiness,
plead for a flashlight to shine a path
through whatever darkness you are facing,
it's like stepping back into the forgotten
church of this one body, and finding all
the stained glass still intact, every pew
dusty but undamaged, just waiting for you
to sit here again in worship, to sing
in praise of the actual heart that has never
stopped working for you, resting only
in the slimmest of instants between beats.
Now place a hand on your chest and
speak—not to the God above but the one
who lives right here inside you.

Our bodies, having endured this great loss, might feel like abandoned churches, neglected for too long and now desperately in need of repair. Whether we pray in more traditional ways to a Creator, or pray through acts of generosity and tenderness, we might make it a practice to include ourselves in our prayers from now on. After I lost my mother and father, it took me a long time to see that I could now give attention and kindness to myself too. Suddenly, there was space for the self I'd left behind in service of looking after them—all the hospital visits, trips to the pharmacy, and so on. There was finally time for me, even if it did not feel comfortable at first.

I believe that any act of self-compassion, no matter how small or large, can help us step back into the forgotten church of the body again. It doesn't make us selfish to tend to our own needs as we turn toward mourning. It's just that we can now see more clearly all the parts of ourselves that were neglected, either during years of caregiving or in the aftermath of loss. I remember one evening just before writing this poem, when I was at home alone, watching a movie that unleashed my grief. Suddenly, reaching for tissues, I realized that I was grieving for myself as well, for the suffering I had endured alongside both of my parents, for the ways I'd had to grow up too soon. I felt a gentle love springing up inside me for the little boy who was afraid to live without his mother and father, and for the man who was afraid to live without the sense of purpose my years of caretaking had given me.

We now have permission to look after ourselves again, to tend to the many layers of this complex pain we will each feel in our own ways. Now is not the time to slip back into old habits of caregiving others or to abandon ourselves to distractions like work. We can ask for our own happiness and for help through whatever darkness we might now be facing. We can ask ourselves for what we need too, placing a hand on our chest to remember that sacredness dwells in each of us. We don't have to look any further than our own hearts to find a church that will always welcome us back.

Invitation for Writing & Reflection: Whether you practice prayer or not, consider writing a kind of blessing for yourself, asking for your own happiness and joy, even if these qualities seem impossible to feel right now. Describe how it feels to bring this small amount of attention to yourself, beginning with the phrase "When I ask for my own happiness" and letting the words carry you forward.

How to Love Yourself

Sit by the open window as long as you can,
listening as rain taps out its own rhythm
on the canopies of trees at last gone to green.
Feel how that music seeps into you
as each new droplet sinks into soil,
touching earthworm and root, feeding
all the small things we cannot see.
This solitude is food for you too,
the kind of love you give yourself
as you would a guest in your home.
Ask: What do you need, how can I help,
the way rain offers itself to the world,
polishing each stone and leaf, before
dropping down into the grateful ground.

There are countless ways to love and care for ourselves in the wake of loss. Yet often the most replenishing acts are also the smallest, like the one I describe here:

simply sitting by an open window and listening as rain begins to fall. This poem came to me on a free day when I decided to indulge in as much joy as I could—getting a long-overdue haircut, driving several hours to my favorite bakery for buttery pastries, taking a miles-long walk on a trail where I could bathe in nature for a while. By the time I got home late that afternoon, I felt more refreshed than I had in weeks. And when I heard those droplets tapping the canopies of trees, I moved my chair closer to the window and just sat there, not only soaking in the soothing sound of rain, but also basking in the fact that I had taken good care of myself all day.

Our grief doesn't go away but can be held instead by such healing rituals. When we say yes to self-love, choosing stillness over busyness, even for just a few minutes, we become like the earth itself, receiving the necessary medicine of rain. It's useful to remember all the small things that might soften our pain and make our days more livable. At a time when clarity seems more abundant, we might write about a moment like this in our journal, when some little act of care allowed us to feel whole and alive again. I also keep a list of things that uplift me nearby, such as walking through a museum, the sound of rain, or a simple cup of tea, since it can be hard to recall what might help us when we're caught in sorrow and despair. But we don't have to worry about getting too lost in our joy either. We do not forget or abandon our loved ones when we partake in the delights and pleasures to which they no longer have access. In fact, the small kindnesses we offer ourselves, as we would a guest in our house, allow us to bring our grief even closer and carry it with more lightness. In a way, we may come to see that loving ourselves is one of the many ways we honor the ones we have lost.

Invitation for Writing & Reflection: Often, we will need reminders to practice self-compassion and perform kind acts for ourselves right now. Write out a set of instructions for how to care for yourself at this moment, whatever that might include, asking yourself what would be most helpful right now. If you decide to write, you might begin with the phrase: "This is how you love yourself" and see what comes.

All I Want

Two decades without him, and all I want
is one of my father's plain white T-shirts
draped over the back of a chair after work,
to trace the map of grease stains and islands
left over from his dried-out sweat.

To feel it peeling off his back as he asks
for another massage, and to give it this time
with full knowledge of how much pain he's in,
without counting down the minutes
on his bedside clock.

                              To see that jade cross
dangling beneath the band of his V-neck
as he bends to tend the tomatoes, to ask
why he dug it out of a flea market box
and started wearing it those last months,
rubbing the stone when he thought
no one was looking.

TURNING TOWARD GRIEF

                    To lift one of his T-shirts
out of the closet where I keep them, and feel
my hand reaching through the cotton weave
to work the knots from his aching back
one last time.

After grief, we often ask ourselves: Why didn't I do more? Why didn't I try harder to save them? In looking back at that time before we lost our loved one, we will often find reasons for guilt or shame. We may feel regret for the ordinary, seemingly forgettable moments we did not stop to appreciate enough. When my father was still alive, for instance, I never really noticed those work shirts he'd shed as soon as he came home, draping them over the kitchen chairs. My father worked long hours as a maintenance mechanic at a factory that made plastic toolboxes until he grew too weak with hepatitis C to keep it up. Now, of course, I'd give anything to time-travel back to our old house some evening, watching as his rusty pickup truck pulls into the driveway, seeing him smile as he throws open the screen door and greets us all, smelling sweetly of grease and sweat.

If I could go back now, of course, I'd do more to care for him, fully aware that he kept the struggles of his illness hidden from us for years. I would not roll my eyes, feeling put out when he asked me to work those knots from his back. And I would not count down the minutes on the bedside clock until I was finished massaging him and could go watch TV again. But that's not what happened.

As we learn to face the pain of our loss head-on, we can try to accept the possibility that we *did* do all that we could, gave all that we had to give at the time. Even if we did not get to say a proper goodbye or resolve our lingering issues with the one we lost, we can try to trust that all is forgiven now. We can choose to believe that our loved one would not want us suffering under the weight of so much regret. It may be useful to explore how we might handle things differently, as the changed person we are now becoming. But maybe the next time we catch our minds reaching back to the past, wishing we could revise what happened and blaming ourselves for not doing more, we can gently say to ourselves: *That's not what happened. This is how it is now.* We can give ourselves grace for being preoccupied (and thus human), for working with our limited knowledge of the private pain of others. Instead of shaming ourselves for what we failed to do or say back then, we can resolve to stay more present, appreciating the people around us and our daily lives in the here and now.

Invitation for Writing & Reflection: If you could go back with the knowledge you have now, how might you change your actions and words with the loved one you have lost? If you choose to write, you might begin with the phrase "This time, I would . . . " listing those things you'd do differently now, perhaps with more presence and loving awareness this time.

Staying Open

Perhaps love begins
with self-forgiveness,
with a gentle wind
that carries the scent
of awakening earth,
and the stronger light
of a sun that seems
to call everything green
to the surface, to meet
each moment of growth
and struggle with warmth,
staying open even when
the sky breaks apart
and rain batters the heart.

Perhaps real love begins when we forgive ourselves for all the perceived wrongs and missteps of the past. We can decide not to see ourselves as broken somehow for not having been able to save our loved one. Instead, we can start to see that our past experiences simply mean we are human too. When we become gentler with ourselves, welcoming regret as part of this journey and setting a place for guilt at the table, it's like a soft wind blows through our lives again, carrying the scent of soil waking up after a long sleep. But how do we practice the self-forgiveness and self-love that allow us to embrace those glimmers of joy when they come, often alongside our grief? We see that there is some stronger light in us that wants to call forth everything living and ready to bloom. And we have a choice as to what we allow our light to touch and nurture. If we keep feeling guilt and fear, more of that will grow. If we keep feeling forgiveness, compassion, and kindness, we will find those green shoots pushing up everywhere as they do in the thawing ground. We cannot keep the struggle and pain out of our lives, but we can meet it with warmth and welcome, discerning which emotions truly deserve our attention.

I wrote this poem out of the darkness of grief for my mother, who died too early, leaving me in a state of shock. For months before her passing, I felt such guilt that I did not listen when she tried to tell me something was wrong or when she asked me to stay with her just a few days longer during one of our final visits. I was traveling for work at the time and felt I could not reschedule the trips I had planned across the country. I told her I was so sorry. "I know," she said, wiping her eyes. "It just hurts."

After replaying her pained words and the entirety of her last difficult year over and over in my heart and mind, finally a gentle wind swept in. I realized how much I had been blaming myself for her death, believing that if I had just stayed with her or visited more often, I could have kept her alive. By writing a letter to myself in her voice and letting this poem flow through me, I learned that I could forgive myself little by little, knowing it would take time and practice. I would have to meet each moment of regret with warmth and let that rain batter my heart for a while, trusting that the storm would soon pass. I would also have to ask myself repeatedly, "What if everything worked out exactly as it was supposed to, even if it did not fit my ideas or plans?"

When facing loss, it can feel like the sky we've always known is breaking apart, disintegrating before our very eyes, the whole world shifting and changing. Yet if we are soft and patient, forgiving ourselves as often as we need to, feeling the pain without adding extra stories, then we will feel the relief of our sorrow lifting for a few minutes, and then perhaps a few hours at a time. We will catch glimpses of our own personal spring, bits of green and the buds of flowers at last pressed to the surface. We might also remember how much rain it takes to make the plants rise and bloom. The way they reveal themselves to this sometimes harsh world, knowing they need the storms and the sunlight in order to grow.

Invitation for Writing & Reflection: Write a letter to yourself in the voice of the one you have lost. Let your imagination run free with this, and don't worry if it feels strange at first. What would your loved one have you know?

Spring Equinox

Looking down at the pink, unlit wicks
of the crocuses, and daffodil buds
swollen but taking their own sweet time,
I wonder if an equinox also occurs
in us during grief, if some personal sun
crosses the equator, as our nights
begin to grow shorter, daylight filling
our lives for longer and longer periods.
These perennials are wise: They sense
sleet, high winds, the shroud of snow
to come. Maybe there are parts of us
that know without our knowing when
it's time to open again—we just wake up
one morning drenched in light
and shivering, forever changed.

There does seem to be an "equinox moment" in grief, when we feel a shift in the balance of brighter and darker days. It may take months or years for this to happen. It may come as a welcome relief. But it does not mean that we ever stop grieving our loved one. It does not mean our heart is not still broken or that we don't still burst into tears at the most inconvenient and surprising of times. We just begin to notice the days growing longer and the stretches of night gradually shrinking. I remember a period when this shift happened in me, when I felt it was time to rejoin the world and find joy again in the work I was doing. It wasn't easy to leave behind my long nights, even when I remembered how much suffering had filled those lonely, confused, sleepless hours. I suddenly stood at the threshold of my own life, shivering and unsure if I could open myself to the larger world and to loving those around me. Having become a new creation in the wake of my loss, how did I know if I could still trust myself?

Even as grief began to morph, I noticed that when I felt most vulnerable or found myself alone in a hotel room on the road for work, waves of grief would pass over me, threatening to overwhelm. At the time, these bouts of weeping and deep feeling seemed like setbacks in the healing process. But luckily, even with the onset of that personal spring, I knew my sorrow would never fully be over. I took it all as a part of the painfully slow process—not of healing from grief but of learning to walk with it beside me like a faithful companion, trusting that it still has important work to do in my life. We may have to wait longer than we ever thought possible, but like the crocuses and daffodils, we will know when it is time to open ourselves again. And if we find the world too much or too cold, unlike the first flowers, we can find ways to retreat once more, renew our strength, and know that we are not failures if we still need to dwell in darkness for a little longer in order to stay true to what we feel. In fact, each grief is our own to hold, and equinox or not, only we can determine when it is time to reach for the light.

Invitation for Writing & Reflection: Describe a moment when you noticed a shift in the heaviness and darkness of your own grief, a sudden turning point, even if it didn't seem to last for long. How did you feel this turn coming on, and what changed in you as you considered rejoining the world, resuming some of the daily routines that can serve as anchors in our healing?

The First Peony

Soon, the rain-slicked bud will be
nothing more than a memory
for the plant, and for me, having
held it in my hand on this gray
May morning, when I looked out
and couldn't resist stepping across
wet mulch and clover to get closer,
to touch the pink seam through which
petals were already bursting to become
something far more extravagant
than necessary—beauty as its own
reason for being. Haven't you, too,
felt the pull toward some brief
opulence, born not out of ignorance
but full awareness of these limited,
time-bound bodies? Doesn't it feel
like the creaking open of a tiny door
the moment the peony finally
decides to bloom?

Can anyone blame us if in the midst of our grief, we choose to surround ourselves with beauty? Or if we pause to notice those small moments when the natural world opens the door of itself to a new season, showing us how we might do the same? In his poem "Rhodora," Ralph Waldo Emerson wrote, "Beauty is its own excuse for Being." In other words, we do not have to justify our desire to focus on only what uplifts us right now, even while still actively mourning the loss of someone so close. Grief comes with many conflicting expectations in our culture, and certain family members and friends in our orbit may have ideas about how we should or should not express our sadness. As we move through this altered time, we have to remember that others' expectations have nothing to do with our need to feel our sorrow as it manifests, and to allow ourselves every bit of goodness when it arrives as well.

Because we have become all too aware of these fragile and time-bound bodies, of our limited time on the planet, we may find ourselves making choices that would have seemed strange to the person we once were and to the people around us. I remember after my father died how I chose to follow my love of poetry and writing, even though it meant making decisions that others often questioned. Friends told me on the phone how much they worried about me moving from place to place, taking part-time jobs that left space for my creativity but little room for much else. Luckily, I knew better than to listen to them; they had not yet lost a parent or close loved one, after all. They did not know how loss strips our life of doubt and pretense, and helps us blaze a trail toward what matters most. I gave up the so-called safety of a steady job, in part because I felt "led" by my father, and by my own pried-open heart, toward the beauty and joy that were still available to me. I had seen how the body of a strong and fearless man can break apart, and had watched as my father lost his battle to stay alive at the very young age of forty-three. I knew I had no choice but to let my own life, my own soul, guide and speak to me.

This was also why on the morning I describe here, I found myself walking barefoot through wet mulch to trace the slow-motion unfolding of the first peony of spring. I wanted to be there for the instant it bloomed, wanted this to be the most important thing to which

I gave my attention. The first spring after I lost my mother, I filled the house with as many flowers as I could—peonies, then daisies and black-eyed Susans, then coneflowers and hydrangeas placed in every vase and jar I could find, decorating every windowsill, where I would see beauty every time I passed by. We may not sense it right away, but eventually, that door will open in us too, and we will feel a blooming, a kind of rebirth that brings us alive again. Even as we lapse back and forth between weeping and delight, grief and excitement, we will see that this new opening, tiny as it is, lets us stay present to the whole experience of our all-too-brief time here on Earth.

Invitation for Writing & Reflection: As you move through the ups and downs of loss, notice how you might be drawn to certain unexpected joys that never occurred to you before. See if you can describe a time when you followed one of these impulses, even if the heaviness of sorrow also came with you. How did you feel your own senses opening up to this bit of beauty you were able to embrace?

Summer Solstice

Peonies bow low to the ground,
petals blown apart and dissolving
back into earth after each rainfall.
Meanwhile, the woodpecker knocks
on the oak door of this summer day,
demanding to be let in. Meanwhile,
the daylily blooms a month early,
orange velvet dusted with a trail
of pollen left by some hurried bee.
And what will we leave behind
when we move on to the nectar
of some other life? I just want to be
remembered as the pond recalls
the shimmer of noon sun, holding
those particles inside its body
as we leap from the dock at dusk.

Loss will leave us feeling raw and almost skinless at times, sensitive to others' moods and attuned to even the slightest shifts in the natural world. More than ever, we may notice changes of all kinds, especially those in nature, of which we, too, are an integral part. We see the blooming, feel the expansion of daylight, and then watch as things begin to fade—the blaze of daylilies, for instance, once so striking and bright, lasting for just a brief time before they shrivel with the heat. As Martha Whitmore Hickman has written, "One of the reasons the death of someone close is so profoundly shaking for us is that it holds up the mirror and says, *You, too.*" We have been reminded of our mortality in no uncertain terms by the absence of our loved one and can no longer deny that we, too, must face the same fate someday. We may feel a sudden kinship with those daylilies and peonies, spilling their petals onto the ground.

This is heavy knowledge to carry with us alongside our pain, and we may sometimes buckle under the burden of its weight. But if we also choose to stay in awareness of our limited time on the planet, we may ask ourselves: How do I want to be remembered? Since the death of my parents, I can say that when I am gone, I want others to recall the warmth and light I tried to bring to this world. We might also ask ourselves: What do I want to remember of my time on Earth? Though I can't say for sure how I will answer at the end, I sense that it is not the suffering and sorrow I will hold on to but rather those times when I surrendered to the moment, looking out at those blown-apart peonies and saying to myself, "Yes, I will live this day as fully as I still can." I will leap from the dock of the pond with my husband at dusk, slipping into that body of water, which keeps its warmth long after the strong summer sun has set.

Invitation for Writing & Reflection: What images come to mind as you consider the changing, blossoming, and fading of the natural world around you? How do you want to be remembered when you're gone, and what very small things might you do today to support that intention? What are you already doing that aligns with how you hope to show up in your life from now on, especially while feeling so painfully aware of our limited time here on Earth?

Compassion

Compassion sat quietly beside me
that December night with my father
in the dim light of his ICU room,
then led me by the hand to the end
of the hallway where I bought him
a cold bottle of Coke, which I placed
sweating on his tray, unwrapping
a straw and bending the end until
it faced him. Now I see it was only
compassion that kept my voice steady
as I said goodbye to him, sensing
it would be the last time, even as nurses
hustled me out, said to go home
and get some rest. Only compassion
that made me linger by his bed,
gripping the callused hand that had
fixed so much for me over the years,
then moving that bottle of soda

a little closer, so he could reach it
once I was gone.

We sometimes place too much pressure on ourselves to say a proper goodbye to loved ones before they leave this world. We may carry deep regret if we didn't get to see them before they passed, if we did not say all that we meant to or share a moment of tenderness together. I was lucky enough to offer one last gesture of love to my father the day before he died. The next morning when we returned to the hospital, he had slipped into a coma from which he would never emerge. After keeping vigil for hours at his bedside, I drove home to shower and change, only to find he was gone by the time I came back. I was grateful for that final act of care—buying him the cold bottle of Coke he desperately craved—and our last "I love you" traded back and forth, but I still felt as if I'd missed something essential by not being present when he transitioned. The same was true of my mother's death. Just a few days after I had left her in the hospital for a work trip, assured by doctors that she was recovering, her heart failed, and I was never able to see her alive again.

Yet I have learned that goodbye is more of a process than just a single moment. True closure often doesn't come until weeks, months, or even years after our loved one has left us. And even friends who were with someone the moment they passed on often tell me that they still ended up feeling like they should have done more for their loved one. Many of us still have this same sense of unfinished business. Perhaps we can lay down the heavy load of our regret that the one we lost went before we had a chance to tell them all that we hoped to. Maybe we can trust that, somehow, they know it all. We might come to see the never-ending journey of grief as one long goodbye that includes all the tears, all the laughter, all the mystery of feeling them still near. The root of the word "compassion" means "to suffer with." This does not mean we take on another's pain or buy into the belief that we must always be suffering in order to mourn properly. Instead, we sit with the suffering of our grief, letting compassion for our loved one as well as for ourselves lead us to a place of greater love. We did all we could for them, and now begins the long process of letting go. We let compassion take our hand and lead us into this land of loss, trusting that the conversation will always go on.

Invitation for Writing & Reflection: What are some of the images and memories that return to you of a loved one's last days? We may often blame ourselves for not doing enough, but you might write down some of the many ways you were able to show up with compassion and gentleness for your loved ones and others during this difficult time.

Gentle

I want to be held by each moment
as the arms of branches cradle a nest,
as the center of that nest, lined with
the cottony seeds of milkweed, creates
a cushion for eggs, for the hunger
of hatchlings. I want to make of each
passing minute a safe place for myself
and everyone around me, twig by twig
building a life that shelters others beneath
my strong wings. I want to seek only
what feeds us, what softens the world—
like thistledown, like clipped grass,
like feathers plucked from the underside
of my own body.

Some days, we may need to be radically gentle with ourselves in the face of this new loss. Even after months or years have passed, we will still have those days when all we want is to be cushioned in the softness of home, when we will need to seek only what feeds us. At such times, we can make a conscious decision to surround ourselves only with the tender, caring energy that will help us heal. This may mean being frank with certain people in our lives—and ourselves—about our desire to be alone, drawing tight boundaries. We might have to leave behind, at least for a while, certain family members and friends who cannot offer us the gentleness that our grief so often requires, perhaps because they want us to become our old selves again or because they want to rush us past our pain. But there is no returning to who we once were when our world has been so altered. There is no speeding beyond the sorrow in which we must dwell for as long as it takes to pass through this portal.

When we can barely function and need to be sheltered, we can remind ourselves that it will not always be this way. For now, we may need a nest of our own making. We may need to be held the way the arms of branches cradle a nest. Others may support us and help hold us up, but mostly, we will need to be soft with ourselves at this time, not layering on any extra judgment, guilt, or self-blame. This is why that final image of the poem remains so central to me. Many birds will pluck feathers from their own bodies to line their nests, knowing how comforting and insulating these feathers are. In that same way, we can give ourselves a soft place to land.

Invitation for Writing & Reflection: Consider the different kinds of gentleness you might need in your life right now. What would feel soft and supportive to you? If you choose to write, try beginning with the phrase "I want to be held by" and see what arrives for you.

To Be Alive

In every moment of grief, there is
a small opening, perhaps the size
of the hole cut in the birdhouse
hung on a tree in my neighbor's yard.
It seems that nothing could thrive
in that tight, dark space, but soon
I see the flash of fledglings aching
for flight, yet still afraid of it.
And when the mother wren returns
with food, somehow fitting herself
through the opening, I hear
the chirping chorus of their hunger
to be alive, and standing alone
on the gravel road, suddenly
remember my own.

At a certain point in the grieving process, we might begin to experience small openings when the hunger to be alive rises up again inside us. We might also weep at times, not always from the pain of our loss but also for the beauty and brevity of this one life our grief has revealed to us. I felt the ache of aliveness on the day I came across a birdhouse filled with winter wrens. I had been struggling through the hours, feeling as unformed and afraid as those fledglings, aching to be a part of the larger world again, yet still not quite ready. As I walked down the road to check the mail, I paused by the birdhouse and saw the mother wren bringing home food for her young. I was there for the instant she shrank her body small enough to fit through the tiny hole, and then heard the shrieking chorus of the fledglings' hunger until she fed each one. It all happened so fast, I almost couldn't believe what I'd just witnessed—this small miracle, this bit of everyday wonder. And suddenly, the world seemed so vivid to me again. I felt my own deep, bodily hunger to be alive, and savor more future moments like this. We can't force wonder to find us, but we can stay available to our surroundings, ready for our moods and thoughts to shift as grief moves through. Some days, we might feel as if we live inside a place as tight and dark as that birdhouse. Yet soon, we get a glimpse of the new life that awaits us when the time is right to reenter it. Even when our sadness returns, as it will, we can hold on to our glimmers and rejoice that a sudden awe for such ordinary things is still possible.

Invitation for Writing & Reflection: What feels most true for you about the journey of loss so far? In your journal or in conversation with a trusted loved one, you might describe some small openings you have noticed and any small victories you can now claim as you move toward life again.

Small Wonder

All week, this loss I can't explain,
empty space at the center
of each new day like a bowl
waiting to be filled. Until I wake
in the middle of the night and rub
what feels like sand from my eyes,
until I make a cup of coffee
in the dark and carry it downstairs
where the smoke alarm starts
to scream and flash for no reason.
Heart startled back into my chest,
I ease open a window and stand
breathing in the late summer air,
its humid kiss on my face.
A breeze stirs the surface
of the birdbath, and that pool
of moonlight and starlight breaks
into sparks as the water
trembles awake again.

We are awakened and made new by times of difficulty, brought back to the truth of our own precious and temporary life. We may be able to name the immediate grief we feel, but often that comes with a series of additional losses we can't quite explain. Perhaps for a long time after a loved one's death, we feel disconnected from any sense of wonder or appreciation for the things in life that once brought us joy. We may feel like the empty bowl I mention in the poem above—hollow, scraped clean, waiting to be filled by something new. Yet sometimes, moments arrive that startle the heart back into our bodies, dropping us down into the center of our lives with eyes pried open. Such was the morning I describe here when, sleepless, I finally rose to make coffee, then carried it down to my office so as not to disturb my husband. As I passed by our bedroom, the smoke alarm in the hallway began to flash and scream as if the whole house were being raided. My husband stumbled out of bed, and we both wondered what on earth had happened—there was no smoke, no fire, no reason the alarm should have sounded just then. Yet I found myself shaken awake. Alone in my office,

I opened the window to breathe some fresh predawn air, trying to calm my racing pulse. And for the rest of that day, I managed to carry this wakefulness with me, this openness to surprise. That false alarm—was it my late mother, father, or one of my grandmothers?—had called me back to the sparks of joy and wonder that come to us when we least expect them, when our eyes have been rinsed clean again, and we have been reminded that our only task is to stay open.

Invitation for Writing & Reflection: Describe a time when you felt jolted awake in some new way during your grief. How did the world come alive for you, even if briefly? You might begin with the phrase "Now, I am awake to" and see what your own sense of wonder sparks in you.

A Slice of Actual Light

And then one day, life placed
a slice of actual light on your plate
instead of the usual portion of grief
you thought would be your daily meal
for the rest of your time on Earth.
You just turned and saw a patch
of winter sun sliding up and down
the wall beside the bed, last gasp
of daylight so inviting, how could you
not reach out and touch the heat
that had slipped through a momentary
crack in the clouds? Now, believe
this will keep happening, these
glimmers gathering to overtake
the long shadow of sorrow for whole
minutes, even hours at a time.

One of the most difficult aspects of being caught in loss, or held in the grips of depression, is that part of us believes it will never end. We worry that the darkness will never lift and we'll never see the light of day again. Yet it can take so little for us to remember that such periods are temporary. The world still calls to us, in blinks and whispers so subtle they are often hard to notice. One such whisper came to me in the first months after my mother's death, in the middle of winter. As I crawled into bed to read before supper, I thought about the long stretch of cold, snowy days ahead, and felt overwhelmed, helpless in the face of my pain. Suddenly, I turned to catch a slice of actual light sliding up and down the wall beside my bed. It was a simple thing—there for a moment and gone in a flash. But reaching out to touch those few weak rays of the setting sun gave me hope that I would not always feel so locked in sorrow. I saw that, eventually, some flavor might return to my days, and I might find a structure that lent purpose to my life again. We may not believe it yet—that more and more, such glimmers will slowly overtake the long shadow of grief—but maybe we can trust in the process of something larger than ourselves. Maybe we can turn toward nature and recall how often the light finds a way through.

Invitation for Writing & Reflection: What small glimmers have startled you awake this week? Have you had a similar experience of being called out of despair or grief, however briefly, by the glimmer of something you simply could not turn away from? If you feel called to write, you might begin with the phrase "And then one day" and see what images or memories come to you.

A Bowl of Hydrangeas

I stand at the sun-struck window
for several minutes longer than I wish,
until I see how the hydrangeas seem
to absorb the light and give it back
even while cut off from the living plant
on which they first came into bloom.
We are like this too in our grief—
separated from loved ones, stunned
and confused, yet glowing with some
new kinship to all things living and dead,
like this cluster of white flowers
I reach out and touch, rubbing petals
between my fingers to remember
I have a body, I am still so alive.

We are like those hydrangeas when we grieve—cut off from the people and things that once fed us, feeling isolated from the larger human community. And yet part of us senses this disconnection is a false one. Part of us keeps seeking the light we need, filling ourselves with it. The more we authentically feel through this unbearable time of loss, the more we might eventually become beacons for others to do the same. I have heard stories from grieving friends who tell me they have found great meaning in guiding others along on this inevitable journey we will all share.

I still remember the autumn day this poem came to me. I had been lying down and reading, glancing up now and then and marveling at the hydrangeas on the windowsill, when a battering wave of grief swept over me, and I began to weep. But this time, it felt different. I found that I was crying for the recent loss of my mother, while at the same time weeping with gratefulness that I was still here, alive to the glowing orbs of those blossoms, to leaves falling outside, to my own head resting on a soft foam pillow. I'd never been able to so easily make room for the impulses of sorrow and joy that can arise from the deepest parts of us, often in the same breath. How could I be feeling both at once?

We will all have moments like this, but we do not need to feel guilty for the gratitude. In fact, we feel it almost as a command—to love others, ourselves, and this world more deeply than we ever have, given the stark reminder of how brief our lives can be. Even simple things, like a bouquet of flowers from the yard, can call us back to our aliveness in all its challenging, blissful forms. Maybe by allowing ourselves to take real physical pleasure in the people and things around us, we are keeping in touch with the ones we've lost too, whether rubbing petals between our fingers and delighting in the satin-like texture of them or feeling the heat of a sun-warmed window beneath our palm. Perhaps we keep loving by letting all of our senses swing wide open, inviting the whole world inside us.

Invitation for Writing & Reflection: Have you experienced an instance of "grateful grief," when you felt the pain of your loss alongside the joy of your own aliveness at the same time? What are some of the ways your own world has felt more vivid in the wake of loss? See if you can stay open to simple moments like the one I describe here, which always bring us back to our bodies and a felt sense of the physical.

Early October

Pink fades from the petals of echinacea
like the scraps of a fraying blouse
washed too many times in summer light.
Now, we are reaching the end of something,
and it's hard to believe these flowers
won't be here in a few weeks, crowding
my window with their silent swaying,
their top-heavy presence. What once fed
butterflies and bees will now dry out
to feed the finches, each heart-center
turning to seeds that will soon disperse
on scouring wind. May it be so
for each of us too, the hidden parts
of ourselves becoming something lighter,
the pieces we finally learned to love
in spite of it all, drifting off
or clamped in a beak, our true essence
spreading across the earth.

TURNING TOWARD GRIEF

There's no escaping the often bittersweet, not-so-subtle reminders of grief that can arrive with the changing of the seasons each year. As we edge toward the anniversary of our loss, and especially as the Earth tips into winter, we might find it hard not to lose ourselves in some new form of mourning. We might see the petals of echinaceas fading from their deep pink to an almost washed-out and tattered white, and feel how we, too, are worn by the passage of time. Yet perhaps autumn can also show us that as we are weathered by life, we can allow the hidden parts of ourselves to become something lighter, our true essence finally revealed. The Japanese, who give language to the ineffable, have a word for this force that resides in all beings—*inochi*, which means "the life-essence that is in everything." Toward the end of both of their lives, my mother and father revealed an irrepressible joy and sense of freedom, despite the pain that weighed them down. We sometimes see this essence in the peaceful look on someone's face as they approach death. And for those of us left behind to grieve, perhaps we feel ourselves weathered and transformed by our loss, worn down to the truth of who we really are.

Invitation for Writing & Reflection: What is feeding you right now in your own season of change and transition? What examples of transformation might you find in the natural world? You might begin by writing the phrase "I am fed by" and repeat as needed.

Like the Trees

You have been waiting for the body to say,
"This is not an emergency, you are safe."
And when it finally does, in a whisper,
you almost don't believe, you can breathe
a full breath again, and then another,
at last trusting the open arms of trees,
even their menacing shadows at midnight.
Now you know everything that grows must
also feel pain, must fear and doubt until they
sense this same quickening, like sap rising
up in the trunk and spreading through
each limb. You have lived as if underground,
but now you are breaking open, breaking
free, becoming so vast and green, you make
a shady place for others to rest in.

There comes a time in late winter in New England when the sap begins to run in the maples, flowing through the veins of the trees once more. It was this image that came to me when I considered what it is like to emerge out of a deep depression or bout of grief, how our bodies reawaken to the world around us. It can feel like living underground when we find ourselves in the grip of despair, but we might need to embrace this new darkness that lets us rest for a while. We might need to say yes to a long stretch of hibernation if we can manage it, retreating from the brightness, noise, and speed of a world that makes little room for pausing or renewal. Even if we stay away for the space of a single day, the shades drawn and our phones silenced, we will come to see our lives in new ways. Held by anxiety for so long, we may need to work hard in order to believe what the whisper tells us: Life is no longer the emergency it felt like when our loved one was ill or in the time after they died. This is especially true if we've been responsible for looking after someone for an extended period. We might feel in ourselves at last what a good friend of mine calls the "unclenching," like a tight fist softening, and our hearts opening to make space for whatever wants to land there now.

It may seem that the lead apron of sorrow will never shift or lift, but eventually—like sap spreading through the frozen limbs of maples—the old blood will move through us again as slivers of sun begin to break through the heavy clouds of our personal winter. I remember walking through the woods near my house, convinced I could sense the new life rising up in the trees, just as a need to engage with the larger world was flowing through me again too. Even as bare branches clattered above in the slightest wind, even as they appeared barren and lifeless, I could see buds pressing up through limbs, ready to burst free at the right moment. This feeling did not erase my grief, but I began to have faith in my own healing. Because I was open to receiving it, I was given a glimmer of possibility, like a single drop of sap weeping from the wound on a tree, and it was enough to show me that a shift was happening, that my season of grief was not over but changing once again.

Invitation for Writing & Reflection: What does it feel like to finally unclench, when the body finally tells you life is no longer an emergency? What allows you to feel safe as you allow grief to move through, ever-shifting, ever-changing? You might begin with the line "This is not an emergency" and see what arises as you write.

Like the Fern

Like a fiddlehead unfurling
on the forest floor, shedding
layers of worn brown leaves
that had once protected it,
we, too, need to keep growing
at our own pace, in our own
sweet time. Unfolding to reveal
the hidden green heart
we always knew was there
waiting for the moment
it finally became too painful
to stay locked inside
the lightless room of a life
that no longer serves us.

This poem was born of a striking photo my husband took years ago. The print lives on the table outside my office, so each day I pass by that perfect shot of a fiddlehead caught in the midst of its own unfurling one spring. You see the green wheel of the frond still loosening, and what looks like layers of brown paper peeling off as the plant reaches out from under its bed of old leaves. In the months after my mother's death, I began to feel like that fern, engaged in my own painful yet necessary transition, suddenly exposed to an altered and now-uncertain world. We feel so raw in the slow rebirth that loss entails, and like the fern, we must say yes to this new life, to the new creation we are becoming. If we hope to survive and thrive, we must gently release the trappings of the old life, which no longer serve us—habits that do not nourish our mind, body, and spirit; people who cannot walk with us in our grief.

In many cases, we may have no choice but to let go of all past selves and ways of being. I still sometimes find myself glancing at my phone, expecting a call from my mother and wondering what she might need today. The grooves of caregiving are worn deep in our hearts and minds, so we can give ourselves a break. It will take some time to unfurl ourselves in this new world of "without." Somehow, seeing that photo of the fern several times a day helps me remember that grieving is a natural and cyclical process, no matter how often I resist, no matter that I would give anything to see my mother's name pop up again on my phone. It will take us much longer than a season to understand who we are now, and perhaps we can take heart in knowing that growth is not only possible but is also happening as we move through every moment, the tightness unclenching, our spirits healing as we open a little further each day.

Invitation for Writing & Reflection: Describe a moment of your own "unfurling," when you felt grief temporarily loosening its grip and could trust that emerging into the light might be possible. What are some of the ways you can let yourself grieve and grow at your own pace?

Tenderness

You know how a half-buried stone
in the yard will clear all the snow
from around itself, little by little,
leaving only a hollow of warmth
and a cushion of moss you want
to rest on, until winter finally ends?
That's how tenderness works in us,
some heat rising up from beneath,
then spreading outward to touch
the lives of anyone who comes near—
slowly, softly, making a safe place
for them to stand in, melting away
the coldness that gathers around us.

When we consider how we want to be treated while in grief, and how we want to treat ourselves, tenderness begins to seem like the only sane response. Given all that we've been through, of course we crave the warmth of gentle people who will not tax our energy. Of course we long for the kind of tenderness that might help melt some of the coldness that has gathered around our hearts. We come away from any authentic connection, whether with a loved one or stranger, with a sense of hope for a future beyond this loss. Talking with a neighbor on the way to the mailbox, or receiving a smile from the clerk at the post office, we might feel ourselves momentarily uplifted, our faith in the world suddenly restored. As the poet Naomi Shihab Nye has written, "Before you know kindness as the deepest thing, you must know sorrow as the other deepest thing." Though we never would have invited grief into our lives, we know it deeply and intimately now. And as we walk with it each day, feeling how sorrow weighs us down like stones in our shoes we can never remove, we learn to accept forms of tenderness and warmth, however they find us. We will struggle at times to embrace the kindness that comes from others or have trouble giving ourselves the grace we deserve right now. Yet when we choose to practice tenderness at every turn, we make a safe, warm place all around us whose heat ripples far out into our world.

Invitation for Writing & Reflection: What image or memory of your loved one comes to mind when you consider the word "tenderness"? What are some of the ways you might practice this kind of slowing down and softening toward yourself and others in your own life?

How to Listen

Listening is a form of worship,
but you don't have to kneel
on the floor with folded hands
or mouth the perfect prayer.
Just open the door of yourself
to another, become the space
they step through to show you
who they are. This is holiness:
two people seated together
on the pew of a park bench,
at the altar of a kitchen table.
Even if no one says a word
for a while, receive the silence
until it's like a new language
only the two of you can speak.

It is a gift when someone shows up wholeheartedly for us, shelving their agendas and unlocking the door of themselves so that we may enter a more authentic place together. We know what it feels like *not* to be seen and heard, to have our pain dismissed by others and perhaps at times by ourselves as well. Yet the mutual practice of deep listening is one of the most healing acts we can offer, because our full presence with someone does the talking for us. Consider the people in your life who will stay by your side even when it's uncomfortable, even when all that's exchanged is silence. I think of my husband, my therapist, and a few good friends, all of whom are unafraid of silences that can stretch so long they become a language all their own. We have lost a sense of ritual when it comes to personal loss and the larger griefs of the world. In our distracted culture, we often look past the possibility of deep listening, perhaps because showing up is such hard work. As we heal, as we integrate the unthinkable slowly into our daily lives, into our bodies and minds, let us seek out those people and places where we will feel most known, far beyond the surface of things. We need therapists, teachers, spiritual directors, priests, chaplains, yoga teachers, meditation guides, life coaches and all the helpers who can serve as examples as we practice listening to each other again, even when we disagree. Anyone who allows us to speak of real things, asking questions and leaving room for answers, becomes sacred to us through the generous attention of their heart. A park bench or couch can become a pew; a kitchen table or favorite hiking trail can turn into an altar we regularly visit with a friend or family member whom we trust to hold our pain—and whose pain we, too, can learn to hold, without feeling the need to fix or mend a thing.

Invitation for Writing & Reflection: Where have you felt most listened to in the midst of loss? Describe a specific time when you connected deeply with another person, and when listening became its own form of worship. You might start with the phrase "Listening is" and allow your intuition to guide you. Going forward, you might also notice those times when you feel most heard and when you are able to hear what others have to say on a deeper level than usual.

How to Comfort Someone

Be the patch of sunlight on the floor
so that as someone comes near
they feel your warmth and can bask in
the subtle glow. Be the clear window
with shades pulled up, and the sparkle
of snow, which holds space for all
that falls into it. Be the water glass
filled at the faucet, then offered
to another in need, and let them
drink and drink until it's time for you
to go, leaving like the slow fade
of the setting sun on a winter day,
traces of pink light spread
like a balm across the sky.

Showing up fully for someone we care about means coming without an agenda. It means cultivating an authentic presence without trying to offer an easy fix. People can sense when we show up with ulterior motives, and these expectations we bring can sometimes harm or disrupt another person's healing and grieving process. I wrote this poem not long after the loss of my mother as a way of reminding myself of the kind of comfort that was most helpful to me. I can still recall those first days after I found out that she had passed away from sudden heart failure, and my husband, Brad, just sat with me, holding my hand. Perhaps the most comforting thing I ever heard came from him, when he said with tears in his own eyes, "I don't half-know what to say right now." It felt like, in that moment, he was becoming the patch of sun on the floor, giving love and warmth and presence without conditions. Saying he didn't even "half-know" what to say felt so honest to me, it was the drink of clear, cold water I needed just then.

When in the middle of our pain, often all we want is for someone to acknowledge it; we crave simple things like glasses of water and a listening ear. And we need someone who will stay until it's time for them to go, leaving as slowly as a winter sunset. Perhaps they will remind us of the beauty and connection that are still available right now but without pressuring us to move beyond what we feel too soon.

I think of visits with my mother when she was sick, when I thought my role was to make everything better for her. I'd show up at her apartment after a long flight and move like a storm through those small rooms—vacuuming, scrubbing the bathtub, cleaning out the refrigerator—tackling all the chores she could no longer do on her own. Yet looking back now, even though all that might have been helpful and necessary, I can see that what my mother really wanted was for me to sit down on the couch with her and hold her hand. She needed someone who would listen and make space for all of her fears and pains without judgment, without feeling that her illness was a burden. Isn't that what we all want and need in the midst of this trying time, someone who will stay by our side for as long as they can, offering simple relief from loneliness, leaving room for us to express all that we feel, no matter how confounding or confusing? And if we don't have someone like that immediately available, we can try our best to be that nonjudgmental, compassionate presence for ourselves.

Invitation for Writing & Reflection: Write your own how-to poem or list, focusing on how you want to be comforted during your time of pain and loss. What specific things have helped you the most, and how might you pass these gifts on to others when the time is right?

In a Friend's Garden
for Kristi Nelson

"I want to be here to see
the poppies open," my friend says,
telling me why she never travels
anymore in the middle of summer.
We each hold one of the heavy buds
whose petals already ache to break
free and spread, bursting red at the seams.
The mulch is warm beneath our feet,
and sunlight shimmers pink in the
shifting leaves of the Japanese maple.
I keep hearing her words—*I want
to be here*—and feel something new
leaning toward the light inside me too,
some seed of need just to be rooted
right where I am for each small pleasure,
every rippling wave of sorrow.
She wraps an arm around me, and we
go inside for tea. There is nothing

to escape from but our own desire
to escape at all.

The desire to escape from our sorrow will at times feel overpowering. We may even want to push away our joy in the wake of this loss, falsely believing that we do not deserve delight or that we are somehow betraying our loved one if we surrender to pleasure. Yet there will come a time when, like poppies in early summer, our joy bursts at the seams, breaking through the heavy armor of grief to show us some brightness that waits on the other side of what we now feel. This will often require us to stay where we are, and embrace what grows in the garden of our heart, in that empty space left by the one we have lost. I can still feel the warm mulch beneath my feet as I walked with a dear friend on a day when my pain felt heavy. I can still see light shining pink through the dancing leaves of the Japanese maple. It was one of those days when enough time had passed for me to drop into the pleasure of the moment, just strolling through a garden with someone I love, while also holding the memory of my mother and the Japanese maple I'd planted in her honor in our own garden at home. We forget that joy and sorrow are the braid we carry inside us each day, the two so woven together they've become indistinguishable from each other. And when we try to escape our sadness, or any other emotion for that matter, we miss out on the moments for which we want to be here—when those poppies finally open, for instance, and the world suddenly seems a more welcoming and beautiful place.

Invitation for Writing & Reflection: What are some of the small things for which you want to be here right now? How might you remind yourself to stay when the mind strays into the belief that some "better" future place or moment waits down the road, beyond this grief and what you are feeling? If you choose to write, you might begin with the phrase "I want to be here for," repeating it over and over, and see what calls to your attention.

Blue-Eyed Grass

All spring long, you have waited
for the tiny, star-shaped flowers
of the blue-eyed grass, glancing
out the window, squinting at that
same place in the yard where they
appear each year. Why do we try
to rush delight, strong-arm joy
into busy lives, when so much
beauty already seeds itself beneath
our restless feet? Why not sit out
on the back porch and watch for
the moment those small beings
blink open their eyes, more violet
than blue in the late afternoon,
awakening some wildness
too long asleep in you?

We might turn to work and other distractions as a way to soften the blows of our grief. And it *can* help to stay busy, finding ways to give our lives purpose when we have lost someone so meaningful. But it's easy to use busyness as an excuse not to feel our sorrow, or the delight and joy that may also slip into our days when some of the pain begins to fade. During my own difficult year of many losses, I waited all spring to see the signs of "blue-eyed grass," their star-shaped, blue and violet flowers. The plant looks just like any other clump of grass, and the blooms stay closed until afternoon, when the light and heat of the stronger sun reach their peak and they finally open. So it can be hard to spot.

It is hard to put into words the relief I felt, not only at seeing these small beings growing wild in our yard but also knowing that my grief had begun to lift enough for me to briefly embrace delights like this again. I don't mean to suggest that I no longer missed my loved ones, but somehow, feeling the season shift also allowed me to trust that things would continue to change for me too. Like the natural world, our grief moves at its own slow pace, unfolding as it must, never to be rushed.

Sitting on the porch and watching the blades of blue-eyed grass sway with the warmer wind reminded me that we can't strong-arm delight or joy either, which show up when we make the time and space to welcome them. Perhaps we can learn not to force anything, but instead simply hold it all when it comes. We may believe again and again that we should not feel joy at all in the face of our loss, that we are not *allowed*. But when those sudden moments of grace sweep down, let's say yes to them, knowing we deserve all the relief we can get from this weight we've been carrying. Why not sit out in nature and let the world call to us in its wild beauty? Haven't we earned the right to savor whatever sweetness we can find right here, beneath our feet?

Invitation for Writing and Reflection: Describe a recent time when some small delight or joy slipped through the veil of sorrow. See if you can re-create the source of your delight in all its specific, sensory detail. How did you feel when the joy came—relieved, guilty, ashamed—or were you able to welcome it fully?

So Much Space for Song

What made the winter wren say,
"This is my home now," as it carried
stick after stick and tufts of grass
to the tractor, shaping a soft place
inside the arm that lifts the bucket?
What gave such a small body
so much space for song, belting out
notes from its perch on top of the seat,
chirping if we get too close to that
hollow where her young are now
hatching, calling out in hunger?
What fills any of us with care enough
to say yes to this difficult world,
taking our places in it, despite
the risks, knowing the dangers?
Watch how the wren shrinks itself
to fit inside the tractor we haven't
driven in weeks, where tiny beings
have just emerged from eggs the size

of marbles, each one filled with
the songs of their mother and father,
a music that's larger than this
one life we are given.

Love means continually saying yes to this rough and difficult world, where what we cherish most must also fade and leave us, where we must mourn the loss of so much. Yet perhaps nature teaches us that our spirits are larger and more resilient than these bodies we were given, and there is still so much space for song, joy, and celebration of the life that remains inside us. I felt this when my husband and I discovered a family of winter wrens living in the most unlikely of places, having made a nest inside the arm of our tractor. It was my first summer after having lost my mother and both grandmothers, and some days I could barely muster the energy to walk outside and feel the sun. Just as soon as I'd feel lost in thought and memory, however, I'd hear the winter wren perched on top of the tractor seat, belting out that morning's irrepressible song. It was so healing to hear that daily music, to be called back to a world I often felt I could not trust anymore. I couldn't help but feel that even as the wrens made a soft place in the tractor for their young, they were also building a gentle place for my own grief to rest in for a while. We didn't drive the tractor for weeks, keeping watch until their young had emerged from their eggs and finally fledged the nest. Yet I couldn't stop asking the question, which remains central to this poem and to my own life, "What gives any of us love enough to say yes to this fleeting world, knowing the dangers, accepting the risks?" We may feel some part of ourselves holding back from life right now, refusing love, afraid of entering the space of grief again. But look at the wrens, so filled with song it bursts forth from them, trembling their tiny bodies. They make nest after nest in the places that seem safest, constantly moving on, drawn by a stronger sense of purpose and devotion. Slowly, gently, perhaps we can start to feel our own purpose stirring again in the simplest of ways—preparing a meal for someone, doing a few chores. Soon, we may see that we, too, can learn to live out in the open, no longer holding back the joy of being alive.

Invitation for Writing & Reflection: See if you can find examples of this same kind of care in the natural world, these efforts to make a "soft place" for small things to grow and thrive in spite of all the dangers and risks. How might you create those soft places in your own life, for yourself and others, especially in this time of loss?

Say Yes

Say yes to suede sandals
you slip on to step outside—
yes to sun on your arms, even
the pink welt of a mosquito bite
rising up to greet you. Say yes
to this clump of wild geraniums
growing in perpetual shade
behind the house, through a rip
in the forgotten blue tarp.
Say yes to tiny pink flowers
winking in the dark you move
deeper into, so that you may
receive their promise: Yes,
they say, you, too, can find ways
to thrive even in those places
where light seems scarce.

Eventually, we may find this sudden new urge rising up in us—to welcome again the everyday experiences of this one life, no longer turning them away. It is one of the most powerful practices I know, saying yes even when we might want to stay hidden, even when things feel unpleasant, annoying, or painful. We can't say yes to everything, of course, but we can try to resist our world a little less with each passing day and embrace the reality of "what is" right now. We probably won't feel grateful for all that's happened to us, but we can stay grateful for what life teaches us, which is its own form of quiet acceptance. I can still remember the day I decided to go outside, realizing that spring had suddenly leapt into summer. Coming upon that clump of wild geraniums rising up through a rip in the tarp I had left in our backyard, I couldn't help but kneel to see the tiny pink flowers swaying and thriving in the shadows. Even in grief, it's an ongoing refrain for me, this amazement at the resilience of plants and animals around us, whether it's the winter wrens we found nesting inside the arm of our tractor or the weeds I recently saw growing on the floorboard of that same tractor, out of the barest hint of soil left behind by my husband's boots. We can make it our practice to find at least a few things to welcome each day, feeling awe alongside our pain. As we slip on our shoes and step out into the world once more, perhaps we can remember the impulse in each of us to love life—saying yes to the light we're given to make the most of those difficult realities, both large and small, which once seemed insurmountable.

Invitation for Writing and Reflection: What are some of the aspects of your own experience right now, pleasant and unpleasant, that you might say yes to? Begin with the simple phrase "Say yes to," and repeat it as many times as needed, allowing your heart and mind to fill in what you might choose to welcome, even when your own light seems scarce.

A Better Place

They are in a better place, we say,
but what if the dead still exist in a world
that is inside this one, living on as the tiny
glimmer I see in the air around me when I
think of my mother's smile or the streetlight
blinking on, shuddering into brightness
as I pass beneath, remembering my father
coming home from work, his rusty truck
bumping along the driveway. What if they
live on in the small face of the wild daisy
and the red breast of the robin lingering
outside my window, pecking at mulch,
pulling a shining worm from loose soil.
What if, as others promise me, my parents
still live in my heart, having taken over
those few rooms, both of them now seated
at a table in the center, laughing again,
their hands wrapped around cups of coffee

whose heat I can feel spreading in my chest
on those days when I miss them the most.

We might grow weary and impatient with the comforts others try to offer us in times of loss. They might say that our loved ones are in heaven now, in a better place, dancing with angels. They might say that our loved ones are everywhere now. No matter how true these words may feel, they can strike us in the moment as insensitive or hollow. We do not necessarily want to be eased out of the grief we need to feel so that it may pass through. Besides, to imply that the one we have lost is all around us now is no real comfort at all—not when we crave their actual touch, the sound of their voice, their physical presence on Earth again. This poem sprang out of my own weariness, having heard one too many times that my mother and father must now live in my heart. I began writing with the intention of sharing some of the odd and mysterious ways they are indeed still with me. The tiny glimmers I see when I am thinking about my mother—her smile, her laughter, her tears. Or the way, in the years after my father's death, I'd be walking beneath streetlights only to have them flicker on quite suddenly as I was filled with the sense that he was near me.

But I was surprised by an image that came to me, of my late parents actually living inside the few rooms of my heart, perhaps chatting over steaming cups of coffee, laughing together again. This image offered me far more solace than any of the well-meaning words uttered by others, as if by imagining my parents together again within me I had somehow made it true. A shift in my grief then occurred, which allowed me to relax and release a little. Perhaps my parents were reunited with each other after over twenty years apart, now held inside my heart. The image also reminded me of a favorite quote by the poet Nikita Gill: "You have turned your heart into a museum of people you've loved to keep them alive inside you." We can't know much for sure about the afterlife, but we can keep our loved ones vibrantly alive inside us, in both heart and mind, by deciding to stay open to the many ways they will surely walk with us in the years to come.

Invitation for Writing & Reflection: How do you feel and stay in touch with the ones you have loved and lost? How did you still sense them near? You might begin with my phrase "What if the dead" and see where the writing leads you.

Strict Diet

Though the doctors said no salt,
salt was all my father craved.
His legs swollen, skin water-logged
and gray, still he wanted potato chips,
honey-baked ham, greasy slabs
of Polish sausage from the deli.
He begged for pepperoni pizza,
garlic butter, ribs slathered in sauce.
But when I did the shopping,
I searched only for labels that said
low sodium and *no preservatives*,
bringing home heads of broccoli,
turkey burgers, shredded wheat.
And when he died anyway,
guilt gnawed me like an ulcer—
how could I have denied him
those few final pleasures?—
until I found Big Mac wrappers
stuffed under the car seat,

jars of pickles in the hall closet,
and hidden among wads of tissues
near the nightstand, his stash:
a half-used canister of salt.
I sat down on his sagging mattress
now stripped of stained sheets
and studied that blue label
with the girl in the yellow dress
holding her umbrella against a rain
of salt falling from the sky.

Food is a universal connector back to our past, back to the loved ones we have lost. We may recall with fondness certain dishes they made, restaurants they loved, or those food and drinks that came to define for us who they were. Meals are one of the few rituals we still observe, giving loving attention to their preparation and arrangement. Food can give us a sense of groundedness and structure at a time when our world has gone off-kilter. For a while after my father died, I felt gnawed by the regret that in trying so hard to be a good son, trying so hard to save him, I ended up also denying my father some of those few final pleasures we might have shared. I have a vivid memory of my twenty-year-old self standing in the aisle of our local grocery store and scanning the labels, feeling dutiful that I was doing my part to help him stay healthy. Imagine my family's surprise then when, a week following his death, we found jars of pickles hidden in the hall closet, burger wrappers in the car, and that salt canister he kept on the floor beside his nightstand. We laughed together through our tears, shaking our heads.

In the years since, I have heard from many others in grief who turn to food as one of the most potent ways to bring their loved ones alive again. It has become a tradition for my husband and me to buy pickles each year around the time of my father's death and eat a few in honor of him. I do the same each summer too, when tomatoes come into season, remembering how much he savored them, always searching farm stands near our house for the perfect homegrown beefsteak tomato. I can still see my father shaking a liberal amount of salt onto each slice laid out on a plate before him. "Brings out the sweetness," he'd say to me when I teased him about how much salt he was using.

Invitation for Writing & Reflection: Are there certain foods that bring back memories of your loved one with a single taste or meals you've shared over the years that especially stand out? Did they have any final cravings? If you choose to write, you might describe a specific recipe or kind of food that you associate with your loved one. How might you use food as a way to honor the ones who have come before, perhaps gathering recipes that offer comfort at this time?

Ember

If my mother's still with me,
let it be the streak of joy
that so rarely passed through her,
burst of laughter like a bolt
of red silk poured into the air.
Let it be her gentle touch,
voice as light as a feather
coasting down on a gust of grief.
If I must miss her, let me
keep some ember of her pain
in my pocket wherever I go
to remember how carefully
we must carry each other,
aware of all that burns inside us.

The idea of carrying a loved one's pain after they are gone might seem counterintuitive to our own healing process. Why would we want to remember the dark times instead of simply holding on to the light of who they were before they left us? Even while grieving, however, we can honor their pain and celebrate the better times as well. Toward the end of her life, my mother did not feel much joy. Especially after the loss of her own mother, with whom she had lived for many years, my mother struggled with loneliness and extreme anxiety. She also lost her sense of purpose, since she was the primary caregiver for my grandmother for a long time, and began to grow depressed. Every few days during the last year of her life, she would call me in distress, understandably resistant to the idea of relocating to a nursing home where she might receive the round-the-clock care she now needed. These conversations, and the final days I spent with her, came back to me in the months after her passing, bringing me to my knees. I felt both guilt and shame for initiating some of those difficult talks, for adding to her stress and fear. I blamed myself for not knowing that she was so close to death.

But how do we ever know? Who wants to see the truth of losing someone so central to our lives? We will all cycle through the process of blame and shame, there is no doubt. We may also feel there was more that health care professionals could have done to save our loved one, to keep them alive and healthy for a little longer. Yet we can choose to carry their pain in a different way too, holding on to the ember of memory—not as a weapon against ourselves but as a reminder that we never truly know the trials of others. Just as we move through our days, running errands, attending meetings, doing what needs to be done with this sorrow in our pocket, and just as our loved one suffered, perhaps not always letting us know the depth of their own pain, everyone carries their unseen burdens. The death of a loved one will not have been in vain if we can allow their suffering to stir a greater sense of kindness and compassion in us.

Eventually, we will hold all the versions of the one who's gone in our heart and mind, able to recall their moments of joy too. We can trust memory to bring back their laughter like a bolt of silk pouring into the air, alongside the tears we must also shed. As the poet Laura Foley has said, "Both joy and sorrow are holy," and they will so often coexist at the same time as our grieving goes on.

Invitation for Writing & Reflection: What are some of the qualities of your loved one that you'd like to hold on to, beyond genetics and family resemblance? What are some of the ways that you carry the one you've lost with you each day?

Pilot Light

My grief lives in the back of my mind
like a pilot light that never goes out,

whether I'm choosing a loaf of bread
in the steamed-over bakery, or throwing

a snowball at my husband, laughing
at the spray of white on the icy street.

Sometimes stifling, other times so welcome
it fills the whole house with its heat.

When our grief breaks, even for a few minutes at a time, like the long and exhausting fever it's been, we can feel grateful to know it will not always be such a stifling presence in our lives. There may even be times that we welcome sorrow, turning toward the warmth of a good memory. Yet in this sudden clarity, perhaps after a day of playfulness, we also see that our grief stays with us like a kind of personal pilot light—always lit, always flaring bright in the center of who we are. I still recall the day I felt my own grief first shifting. My husband and I had gone away for a few days to escape the heavy sadness that hung over our house like a veil of fog. Staying in a new place, walking unfamiliar city streets, I was able to briefly leave behind the guilt and regret I felt around losing my mother.

Even tossing the snowball at my husband and laughing for what felt like the first time in months, I was surprised to find my grief still with me, like the set of house keys that comes along in my pocket wherever I go. Though it was the slightest opening, the tiniest crack, this moment showed me I would not always be trapped in the darkness of loss. I saw how our sorrow accompanies us in the deepest of joys, and we do not forget or abandon our loved ones when we give ourselves over to some small relief. We never relish the pain that brings us to our knees or fills our eyes while out in the world, but we can welcome its presence as further evidence of what most of us already know is true—our love does not die with the person we've lost. Instead, it expands and rises like heat, filling the whole house when we most need to know that love is still there.

Invitation for Writing & Reflection: Pause and give your whole attention to something or someone that calls to you today, taking in the fullness of the scene and waiting before moving on again. It might be something as simple as the steamed-over window of a bakery or the beauty of a street softened by fresh snow. As you exhale into a sense of expansion, what do you notice all around you? What do you notice in your body? Can a sense of peace or joy coexist with your grief, even for a moment or two?

For Now

We walk the sun-struck hayfield,
boots crunching through ice where
snowmelt has pooled and refrozen,
the blades of grass made so brittle
by the bitter cold, they shatter
with each step, like blown glass.
There will never be a perfect moment
when we feel complete, our needs
finally met, and the noise of the mind
falling away like an old furnace
kicking off. For now, light strikes
bare skin, warming our faces as we
walk with the sound of breaking
beneath our feet, learning to hear it
as a kind of background music,
like fear and doubt, which never
quite die down in us, no matter
how bright the day becomes.

As we walk through the winter of our grief, we will likely find a whole chorus of emotions filling us too—fear and doubt, anxiety and anger, maybe even delight and joy at odd moments. This is our new background music, these voices and urges and worries accompanying us everywhere we turn. Our loved one's death has brought us into a state of heightened awareness, of undeniable sensitivity to the world around us, whether we're back at work or taking a walk with a partner or friend. We may now feel on high alert for the slightest shifts in routine, watching for changes in the ways that others treat us and how they do or do not show up to support us. For a while, everyday life can feel like stepping across broken glass or brittle ice—never quite finding our footing, never quite knowing where we stand. Perhaps it is enough to know that every jagged emotion that comes up is to be expected at this chaotic and jumbled time. So much of our lives might once have seemed predictable, with a set of formulas or instructions for how to proceed. But this is not the way of grief. For this reason, I do not find it at all helpful to talk of stages of mourning, or to trace particular phases of the healing process, which is, by nature, different for everyone.

I remember, for instance, after a particularly difficult loss, feeling afraid each time my husband would leave in the evening to visit with friends. I didn't yet feel up to social occasions, but the idea of being left alone with my own spiraling emotions for hours filled me with dread. Then, just a few weeks later, I'd find myself wishing for solitude and space. There is no way to control or predict what we will need on a given day, so we must stay as present as we can to what arises, letting our loved ones and partners know what we are feeling when we feel it, bringing them into our process when it feels right. We will have to ask for their patience (and practice it ourselves) with this temporary Jekyll and Hyde personality of ours, trusting that while we will never be the same, our emotions *will* someday regulate and equalize, and we will feel more like ourselves. Until then, we walk this broken landscape accompanied by the whole spectrum of human emotion, knowing just how universal this journey is.

Invitation for Writing & Reflection: See if you can name your own background music of emotions at this moment in your grief. When you feel especially overwhelmed, tired, or confused, try going for a walk by yourself or with a trusted loved one, and notice all that comes up, perhaps even sharing with your companion as the emotions morph and shift. What images come to mind as you consider the landscape of your own loss? How is it feeling right now for you to move through your life as this changed person?

The Clearing

At the center of every fear
is a clearing, and though you must
trudge for miles in the dark woods
to get there, it's worth the trip:
Now you can sit down for a while
among grass and hawkweed, you can
bask in unfiltered light, and see
the heavy clouds shifting overhead.

At the center of every fear,
if felt completely, is an empty
space where the wind tickles
the hairs on your neck, then arcs
an arm around your shoulder,
pulling you closer like a father
at last unafraid to show affection,
here to let you know you're not alone.

If loss has any purpose at all—and we may feel right now that it has none—then it might be to lead us more deeply into our lives, into our own healing. Death has a knack for revealing to us exactly what we most care about, what we now know we can't stand to lose in the future. Stillness and peace may feel welcome when they arrive, almost like a loved one curving an arm around us to show us that we are not alone in our journey. Yet they often come on the heels of deeply feeling our sorrow, trudging through those dark miles to get to the clearing it can be hard to believe waits inside us. I remember, in the months after my mother's death, deciding to practice self-care by scheduling a massage. As the therapist worked the many knots and blockages from my body that had been wracked by grief, I found, beneath that pain, a disturbing layer of fear I had not encountered before. Now that I had lost all of my grandparents and parents, and many other close family members as well, the person I felt most afraid of losing was my husband.

As I lay there face down, playing out the scenario of his death in my mind, tears streamed from my eyes, and the crying lasted for an embarrassingly long time as the therapist kept up his work. But I knew I had to feel this fear—certainly not brand-new but now more palpable and real to me. Afterward, even though I knew I'd be walking with this unimaginable possibility for the rest of my life—that my husband might die before me—I found a sense of calm I hadn't felt since before my mother's passing. Oddly enough, I was able to sit with my grief in a new way, settled enough to rest more fully, perhaps because I had gone to the center of what made me most afraid and had come to know it a little. It was no cure, of course. I wept again later that day and the next and the next, but at least I knew I could reach that clearing; at least I could trust that some space was often waiting inside the agitation, once the pain had passed through me like a storm.

Invitation for Writing & Reflection: What fears, irrational or not, have you encountered in the wake of your loss, and how might you allow yourself to turn gently toward them or share them out loud with someone you can trust not to judge? You might also find it helpful to write down your fears as they arise in a journal, since acknowledging and naming them often diffuses their power over us. If you could believe that some clearing waited for you at the center of your fear and pain, what would that look like to you? How would it feel to sit down and rest in that calm center, when it finally comes?

Scarlet Tanager

> Moving on is the hardest part
> of loss. As the months add up,
> you realize you will love again
> your one strong cup of coffee
> each morning, even looking forward
> to the dribble of cream. You will
> smile and laugh and feel amazed,
> as the dead cannot, by the sight
> of a scarlet tanager flashing between
> tree branches, then vanishing
> before you can even say its name,
> leaving a faint imprint of color
> on the otherwise ordinary air
> to remind you what once was there.

Is moving on the hardest part of the grieving process, sometimes as painful as those terrible first days after we lose someone? It's difficult to say since grief is unique to each of us. Yet if we do find ourselves feeling guilty, heavy with a new kind of sorrow as we begin to integrate this loss into our lives, we can know we are not alone. We might even remind ourselves, as we feel the larger and smaller pleasures of life gathering around us again—a creamy cup of coffee or the rare sighting of a scarlet tanager in trees beside a road—that our loved ones would *want* us to embrace these joys, no matter how slight, no matter how long they last. Such reengagement with everyday life, with all its ups and downs, might also underscore for us what is most important to us during our limited time on the planet. Do we want to rush through the days of our lives, caught in thoughts and worries about the future, about how to get ahead? Or do we want to remember to slow down and pause for the bright beacon of a tanager, inhaling the steam of a cup of coffee, letting our world imprint on us by staying present to it all just a little longer? Perhaps this practice of pausing will also reveal the imprints our dead have left behind in us too—not quite tangible or physical but present nonetheless, affecting how we treat each new moment, coloring the very air we breathe.

Invitation for Writing & Reflection: What would you say has been the hardest part of loss for you? You might begin by writing "The hardest part of loss is" and see what arrives for you. If you write, you might also choose to describe a moment when you were able to stop and appreciate some seemingly small thing, even while holding your grief close at the same time.

Only Moments Matter

> Only moments matter—not some
> distant future or glittering destination.
> Not the swollen bank account,
> a lake house, or the perfect spouse.
> Only this instant spinning toward you
> today while you sit on a bench
> in the mudroom, taking off your shoes
> and watching the lit-up planets
> of dust dance in the air, each mote
> a moment from your life you hope
> to hold on to, all of them now
> revolving around you—their sun,
> their center, their blazing source.

We can wait for moments to arise in our lives that have the outer appearance of holiness, or we can stay open enough that even the most ordinary moments can shimmer with depth and possibility. Perhaps this immersion in our sorrow has taught us this lesson more than anything else—that every moment spent alive on the Earth is just as sacred as the next. We now see, more than ever, that the purpose of a life well-lived is not just to gather status symbols and actual wealth, or to create formulas for how we must spend our days. Having lost both of my parents earlier than most, I know—and try my best to remember—that only moments matter. Given our mortality and the fragility of all human life, why not make it a practice to face each instant fully when it comes, not turning away toward busyness or the pursuit of worldly things. We still have to pay the bills and change the tires, but we can turn even the plainest hour into a paradise if we surrender to it. We may not be able to explain why a certain moment feels transcendent to us, just as I can't quite capture why the moment I describe in this poem stayed with me long after it passed. I was just sitting in the mudroom, the rugs strewn with bits of gravel and grass clippings, when suddenly, I looked up to see a galaxy of dust, loose hair, and even the squiggle of a tiny blue thread all spinning around me. Because I was not in a hurry to do anything else, I just sat there and watched as my breath stirred all those bright motes in the air. I thought of my parents, grandmothers, and all the people I have lost over the years, all those shared moments that still trail me wherever I go, like unseen dust in the air I breathe. What if our most sacred moments follow us like this, caught in our orbit, lit by the quiet reverence that makes them come alive again?

Invitation for Writing & Reflection: Can you think back to a moment that has followed you across time, and which now feels more sacred in the face of this new loss? Try re-creating the specific details of that memory, with a fuller awareness now of what is most important to you.

Glimmers

Watch for glimpses and glimmers
that ripple through this world so fast
they come like gusts of wind, parting
the seed-heads of rye grass, turning
a field into the sea as you pass.

Find delight in the slight flutter
of a mottled red leaf floating raft-like
in the birdbath—a sign that you are
not alone, that the ones you've loved
and lost are still reaching through

from the other side to stay in touch.
Feel them close by in each rustling
of the rusted-out cinnamon fern
when nothing else stirs, or in a sudden
turn of clouds that allows the sun
to pour through bare trees like honey

pulled from some unseen hive,
spilling everywhere at your feet.

"Joy is not made to be a crumb," Mary Oliver once famously wrote. But sometimes, crumbs—little glimmers—are all we have, especially in the midst of a grief that can still feel fresh even months or years after the fact. It's true, we want to stay open to the rush of sudden delight and deeper connection, but if we are still immersed in our sorrow—as perhaps we should be—life may only send us little messages, like notes slipped under the door of the heart. Before writing this poem, I had tried everything to lift off the darkness that seemed to cling to me, but nothing would work. Then, as I walked through the woods, wondering if wonder would ever find me again, light poured through the bare branches for a few seconds, spilling everywhere across the winter-brown grass at my feet. A bit of sweetness had come to me from nowhere, had slid beneath my awareness to touch some clear place in me. It was enough to bring a weak smile to my face, a hint of amazement at what had happened just when I thought nothing would help. It was enough to feel the deeper presence of something I can only call *spirit*, stirring in the birdbath, rustling the rusted-out cinnamon ferns, even when no wind seemed to blow. The message was: You are not alone in this. And I trusted that truth as the gray day wore on, as I looked ahead to a new year I hoped would be filled with more of these tiny glimmers, these slivers of hope that save us.

Invitation for Writing & Reflection: Write your own list of "glimmers" as they come today, not leaving out a single crumb of the joy you feel. You might begin with the phrase "Just when I thought nothing would help" and see what moments beg to be remembered.

Sweet Mystery

Perhaps you have felt it too,
stepping into an empty room
and knowing the one you've lost
waits in the weave of the carpet,
in the slant of the sun strumming
each leaf of the spider plant until
it seems to hum in the brightness.
A fleeting sense maybe, and yet
when we choose to believe, what
comfort to feel they are still with us,
seated in a favorite place on the couch
and watching the echinaceas ease
open their pink petals in the garden,
the flowers able to hear whenever
a honeybee flies near, and in that
moment of deep knowing, decide
to sweeten their nectar, so the bee
will return again and again.

Given all the mysteries and wonders of our world, perhaps we can give ourselves permission to believe that our loved one is near every time we sense their presence. They may no longer be here in the physical realm, but who are we to say that they don't return to us in some way, shape, or form we can't predict, even if it's something as simple as a feeling that we are no longer alone in an otherwise empty room. In the months after my mother died, sometimes in the moments of my deepest pain, I would feel what I can only call a second presence with me, as warm and inviting as sunlight strumming the spiny leaves of the spider plant, as comforting as the fleece blanket I wrapped around me on cold nights. My logical mind would try and kick in—how can she possibly still be here? Why torture myself with this irrational thought? But eventually, some wiser part of me would chime in: Why not believe? What does it hurt?

We are so caught up in the so-called logic of what's physically possible that we can lose sight of the power of our intuition to *know* what is true, and what is real for us in our grief. If flowers can hear when pollinators are flying near, as scientists have now discovered, if they can respond by sweetening their own nectar, can't we, too, decide to welcome our own visitations, strange occurrences, and serendipities that suggest our loved one has not left us completely? If you talk to anyone who's faced great loss, many will tell you stories of sweet mystery about the ways a loved one keeps showing up in their daily lives. We might call these "winks" from the other side and receive the brief relief they offer us with an open heart and mind, no matter our own spiritual beliefs about a Creator and afterlife. We can perhaps learn to stretch our ideas of how the dead might weave themselves into our days, whether with a phrase they often used, or a song on the radio, or a simple feeling we agree to no longer try and explain away.

Invitation for Writing & Reflection: The next time you have a feeling that your loved one is near even though they are no longer here, breathe in for a moment and decide to believe. How have they come to visit you this time? What sweet mysteries have you encountered since your loved one died, and what things might you choose from now on not to simply explain away?

Ache of Aliveness

I feel it while scuffing through
the first leaves to blanket the garden,
feel it in sun that lifts the dew
from grass blades and fern fronds
beginning to rust at their edges.
I feel it in the thimble of a black
raspberry dangling just for me,
in the way my husband winces
and grips his lower back as if
touch alone could calm the pain.
But there is no cure for the ache
of aliveness that runs like a current
through each of us—we can only
embrace it, bittersweet as the last
ear of sweet corn pulled from the pot,
so golden and packed with sugar
I almost can't bear to bite into
all that long-gone summer light.

With each new transition, we may feel more than ever before the ache of our own aliveness, the bittersweetness (and devastation) of having outlived those loved ones we thought we could never do without. In the wake of our pain, we might experience every shift as a cause for alarm or sudden emergency. But eventually, our emotions will modulate, and the rawness we feel each time we step out into an ever-changing world will settle into a kind of vulnerable aliveness to everything—the highs and lows, the delights and disappointments, the grace and grief—as wild and uncontrollable as nature itself. The ache returns to me each autumn in my part of the world. As the season inches toward winter, I am reminded of the passing nature of all living things—the browning grass, the rusted ferns, even the pulled muscles in my husband's back, which are evidence of our changing, aging bodies. When things turn difficult, we may take heart in knowing that woven in with our sorrow, anger, and frustration is this undeniable current running through each of us. It's a kind of electricity of spirit that, when we tap into it, keeps us connected to each other and the larger world.

Sometimes, we might feel the ache in something as simple as the last sweet corn of the season. Feasting on those kernels packed with sugar, we can hold close the fact that this, too, will soon be gone, while also closing our eyes to savor the taste of what's still right here.

Invitation for Writing & Reflection: What specific aspects of your life right now allow you to feel "the ache of aliveness"? You might start with "I feel it in" and keep repeating the phrase as you fill in all that gives you this sense of wistfulness for what's still right here but will someday fade or change.

Mother Light

In the glow of the porch lamp,
a few shadowed snowflakes fall
and the history of tenderness
glints at the center of each one.
A year ago, the terrible call—
my husband's eyes telling me
what had happened before I even
pressed the phone to my ear
and heard the words: *She is gone.*
Now, I stand at the window tracing
the slow way snow gathers on top
of Queen Anne's lace gone to seed,
until it's like a second bloom
of shimmering white held up
to the night sky—her light still
finding its way to me across
the countless miles between us.

We might find the light of our loved one lingering in some of the most surprising places. But our thoughts will likely turn to them most often on certain anniversaries—birthdays, holidays, the day of their death. When I wrote this poem, it had been a year exactly since I lost my mother. Saying goodbye to her has been the hardest thing I've ever had to do so far, and some days, the pain still overwhelms me. Yet I remain grateful for a writing practice that has helped me express the mysteries, confusions, and cycles of grief, that has allowed me to integrate this new reality into a world forever changed by her absence. I have appreciated the way others have reassured me that my mother is still with me, somehow nearby, and there have been too many inexplicable visitations and encounters not to trust that this is true. The fact is, I feel her close to me much more often than I ever would have expected. But the paradox of grief is that even as we feel our loved ones are as close to us as our next breath, we also feel their distance. Even if they live on in our hearts, or somehow with us in the everyday world, we will always prefer to have their actual, physical presence. As I stood at the window that winter night, looking out at the Queen Anne's lace piled with snow and glancing up at the constellations, which shone so clear in the cold, I began to feel that the love of those we have lost is like starlight. It still travels toward us from places we can't fathom, their love still present and real, even as we know those far-off stars have already burned out.

Invitation for Writing & Reflection: Describe a time in your loss, perhaps during a difficult holiday or anniversary, when you were comforted by the presence of daily things, and when you felt the love of someone still making its way toward you, even though they are no longer a part of this world as we know it. How has the light of their love followed you, even after their death? And how might you carry that light into your own life, turning toward what brings you most alive?

Acknowledgments

The author wishes to thank the following publications and editors in which these poems appeared, sometimes in different form:

"New Year," "Blue-Eyed Grass," and "Finding My Mother" in *Vox Populi*, edited by Michael Simms.

"Space for Song" in *Rattle*, edited by Timothy Green.

"Wound" and "Scarlet Tanager" in *The Raft*, edited and curated by Phyllis Cole-Dai.

"All I Want" in *The Sunday Poem* by Gwarlingo, and in *Plume Poetry*, edited by Daniel Lawless.

"Compassion" in *Poetry of Presence II: More Mindfulness Poems*, edited by Phyllis Cole-Dai and Ruby Wilson.

ACKNOWLEDGMENTS

"A Slice of Actual Light" in *The Wisconsin Poets' Calendar 2024,* edited by Jeanie Tomasko.

"A Better Place" in *Cultural Daily,* edited by Bunkong Tuon.

"Strict Diet," in *American Life in Poetry,* edited by Ted Kooser, Poetry Foundation.

"Ordinary Evening" in *Love Is for All of Us: Poems of Tenderness & Belonging from the LGBTQ+ Community & Friends*, edited by James Crews and Brad Peacock.

"Phone Call" is dedicated to Kim Hays.

"A Slice of Actual Light" is dedicated to Lila Daut and Allen Jacobsen, with thanks for their enthusiasm in sharing this poem so widely.

Endless gratitude to the wonderful team at Broadleaf Books that made this book possible, especially editors extraordinaire Lisa Kloskin and Lil Copan, who first approached me with the concept. Thanks to Gareth Esersky for making so many connections and keeping the Idea Factory going. I'm grateful to Kristi Nelson for her friendship and for the use of the quote from her

ACKNOWLEDGMENTS

article, "Embracing the Great Fullness of Life," published on Grateful.org, as the epigraph to this book.

Thanks to the following friends and loved ones who have directly inspired or supported the poems in this book: Julia Alvarez, Kimberly Blaeser, Barbara Crooker, Laura Foley, Donna Hilbert, Karen Kassinger, Alix Klingenberg, Ted Kooser, Annie Lighthart, Kristi Nelson, Mark Nepo, Naomi Shihab Nye, January Gill O'Neil, Ann and Duane Peacock, Diane Peacock, Erin Peacock, Andrea Potos, Kim Rosen, Ellen Rowland, Patricia McKernon Runkle, Marjorie Saiser, Heather Swan, Rosemerry Wahtola Trommer, Connie Wanek, Diana Whitney, Michelle Wiegers, and Claire Willis.

I am also beyond grateful to my husband, Brad Peacock, who is my first and best reader, and who's been a patient, loving companion throughout my grief journeys thus far. I would not be the poet or human that I am without him.

Notes

68 *In his poem "The Rhodora":* Ralph Waldo Emerson, "The Rhodora," from *Ralph Waldo Emerson: Collected Poems and Translations* (Library of America, 1994), 31.

72 *As Martha Whitmore Hickman has written:* Martha Whitmore Hickman, from *Healing After Loss: Daily Meditations for Working Through Grief* (William Morrow, 1994), entry for July 26.

112 *As the poet Naomi Shihab Nye has written:* Naomi Shihab Nye, "Kindness," from *Everything Comes Next: Collected and New Poems* (HarperCollins, 2020), 222–223.

141 *The image also reminded me:* Nikita Gill, "Your Museum-Shaped Heart," from *Your Soul Is a River*, 2nd ed. (Thought Catalog Books, 2016), 63.

149 *As the poet Laura Foley has said:* Laura Foley, "Joy and Sorrow," from *Sledding the Valley of the Shadow* (Fernwood Press, 2024), 83.

172 *"Joy is not made to be a crumb":* Mary Oliver, "Don't Hesitate," from *Devotions: The Selected Poems of Mary Oliver* (Penguin Books, 2020), 61.